Arthur W. Pinero

The Amazons

A Farcical Romance in Three Acts

Arthur W. Pinero

The Amazons

A Farcical Romance in Three Acts

ISBN/EAN: 9783744769488

Printed in Europe, USA, Canada, Australia, Japan

Cover: Foto ©ninafisch / pixelio.de

More available books at **www.hansebooks.com**

THE AMAZONS

A FARCICAL ROMANCE
In Three Acts

By ARTHUR W. PINERO

LONDON: WILLIAM HEINEMANN
MDCCCXCV

Copyright 1895
All rights reserved
Entered at Stationers' Hall
Entered at the Library of Congress
Washington, U.S.A.

INTRODUCTORY NOTE

ALTHOUGH "The Amazons" was presented to the public a couple of months earlier than "The Second Mrs. Tanqueray," it was actually a later work; indeed, Mr. Pinero may be said to have written this merry and fantastic little play by way of relaxation after the more serious mental effort involved in the composition of the famous drama which told the tragic story of Paula Tanqueray. Curiously enough, this delightful "farcical romance," in the writing of which Mr. Pinero was apparently prompted by no more weighty motive than the indulgence of his own playful fancy, for all the amusement it was worth, stands in order of composition immediately between "The Second Mrs. Tanqueray" and "The Notorious Mrs. Ebbsmith." It may thus be regarded as a remarkable evidence of its author's versatility. Here he attempted no criticism of life, he sought to solve no problem of morality, sociology, or psychology; he merely permitted himself to dally with the "mannish-woman" idea in the lightest, gentlest spirit of satire, and in a most whimsical mood of

INTRODUCTORY NOTE.

Romance. In the Tangle of Overcote Park we seem to hear distant laughing echoes from the Forest of Arden, and in Lady Noeline Belturbet and Barrington, Viscount Litterly, we fancy we recognise the descendants of Rosalind and Orlando.

Mr. Arthur Chudleigh produced "The Amazons" at the Court Theatre on Tuesday, March 7th, 1893, when its reception at the hands of the public was very cordial. The following is a copy of the first night programme:—

Programme.

ON TUESDAY, MARCH 7th, 1893,
WILL BE ACTED FOR THE FIRST TIME

THE AMAZONS
An Original Farcical Romance.

BY

A. W. PINERO.

GALFRED, EARL OF TWEENWAYES	Mr. WEEDON GROSSMITH.
BARRINGTON, VISCOUNT LITTERLY	Mr. F. KERR.
ANDRÉ, COUNT DE GRIVAL	Mr. ELLIOTT.
Rev. ROGER MINCHIN	Mr. J. BEAUCHAMP.
FITTON (*A Gamekeeper*)	Mr. W. QUINTON.
YOUATT (*A Servant*)	Mr. COMPTON COUTTS.
ORTS (*A Poacher*)	Mr. R. NAINBY.

INTRODUCTORY NOTE.

MIRIAM, MARCHIONESS OF CASTLEJORDAN	Miss ROSE LECLERCQ.
LADY NOELINE BELTURBET } *Her Daughters.*	Miss LILY HANBURY. (*By Permission of Mr. Beerbohm Tree.*)
LADY WILHELMINA BELTURBET	Miss ELLALINE TERRISS.
LADY THOMASIN BELTURBET	MISS PATTIE BROWNE. (*Her First Appearance in England.*)
"SERGEANT" SHUTER	Miss MARIANNE CALDWELL.

The scene is laid first in "The Tangle," an overgrown corner of Overcote Park, and afterwards at Overcote Hall. Great Overcote, as everybody knows, is a two-hours' railway journey from town. The events of the play occur during a single day in a fine September.

The scenery is painted by Mr. T. W. Hall.

The music in the Play has been composed by Mr. Edward Jones.

"The Amazons" ran at the Court Theatre until July 8th, by which date a hundred and eleven performances had been given, a record which spells success, although it does not equal the figures of Mr. Pinero's robuster and less fantastic farces, such as "The Magistrate," "The Schoolmistress," and "Dandy Dick."

A successful tour of the provinces was made under the auspices of Mr. Fred G. Latham and the late T. W. Robertson, while at the Antipodes considerable prosperity has attended the merry little play, Messrs. Brough and Boucicault having been its Australian

INTRODUCTORY NOTE.

The greatest success, however, yet achieved by "The Amazons," has been in America. Mr. Daniel Frohman produced it quite unostentatiously at the Lyceum Theatre, New York, and its triumph was immediate. The freshness, delicate humour, and unconventionality of the piece, and the quaint prettiness of the girls' masculine attire, captivated the playgoers of New York, and "The Amazons" became the talk of the town. Presented first in February, 1894, it ran for eighteen or nineteen weeks in New York, the demand for seats being so great as to justify the management in raising the prices in certain parts of the house. Similar popularity has accompanied the piece throughout the United States, where it is about to commence its second season "on the road."

MALCOLM C. SALAMAN.

LONDON, *June* 1895.

THE PERSONS OF THE PLAY

GALFRED, EARL OF TWEENWAYES
BARRINGTON, VISCOUNT LITTERLY
ANDRÉ, COUNT DE GRIVAL
REV. ROGER MINCHIN
FITTON (*a Gamekeeper*)
YOUATT (*a Servant*)
ORTS (*a Poacher*)
MIRIAM, MARCHIONESS OF CASTLEJORDAN
LADY NOELINE BELTURBET ⎫
LADY WILHELMINA BELTURBET ⎬ *Her Daughters*
LADY THOMASIN BELTURBET ⎭
" SERGEANT " SHUTER

The Scene is laid first in " The Tangle," an overgrown corner of Overcote Park, and afterwards at Overcote Hall. Great Overcote, as everybody knows, is a two-hours' railway journey from town. The events of the play occur during a single day in a fine September.

THE AMAZONS

THE FIRST ACT

The scene represents a thickly-wooded, overgrown corner of Overcote Park. There is a small clearing up to a dense thicket and a ragged hedge, which is broken by an old five-barred gate, while prominently in the foreground are, on the left the stump of a felled tree, and on the right an old tree with a wide hollow in its trunk. Beyond the gate is a prospect of a woodland, pierced by gleams of bright light. It is a fine, warm morning in September; some golden leaves are on the trees, a few have fallen. The whole scene is warmly coloured and poetical in suggestion.

YOUATT, *an aged servant in livery, opens the gate for the* Rev. ROGER MINCHIN, *who advances on to the clearing.* MINCHIN *is a type of the country parson of the old school, white-haired, red-faced, hearty in manner.*

MINCHIN.

No sign of her ladyship here, Youatt.

YOUATT.

We'll find her, Mr. Minchin.

MINCHIN.

[*Wiping his brow.*] Ouf!

YOUATT.

[*Closing the gate.*] My lady and the family are very partial to the Tangle o' fine days.

MINCHIN.

The Tangle?

YOUATT.

That's what the family call this corner o' the park, sir. [*Looking off and removing his cap.*] 'Ere is my lady.

MIRIAM, MARCHIONESS OF CASTLEJORDAN, *approaches, carrying a camp-stool. She is a tall, splendidly handsome woman of middle-age.*

LADY CASTLEJORDAN.

[*Shaking hands heartily with* MINCHIN.] Mr. Minchin!

MINCHIN.

How are you?

LADY CASTLEJORDAN.

You so seldom come to see me. Shall we walk back to the Hall?

MINCHIN.

[*Puffing.*] If you don't mind, I——

LADY CASTLEJORDAN.

Get your wind — certainly. [*To* YOUATT.] Has Shuter gone to the station to meet Lord Noel?

YOUATT.

I b'lieve so, m'lady.

[YOUATT *goes away through the gateway*

LADY CASTLEJORDAN.

Well! I see what you're thinking about.

MINCHIN.

Lord Noel—that's Lady Noeline?

LADY CASTLEJORDAN.

From your point of view, yes.

MINCHIN.

Oh, dear, oh, dear!

LADY CASTLEJORDAN.

Noel has been staying with Mrs. Vipont in town for some weeks. The Viponts have been kept in London, you know, by the late session. I've missed Noel sadly. [*Referring to her watch.*] He will be at the Hall in half an hour.

MINCHIN.

Will *he!* And your two other gir—boys?

LADY CASTLEJORDAN.

They spent their August in Scotland; they've been home some days. [*Walking about restlessly.*] It chafes me so to think I am not at the station myself to meet my eldest son.

MINCHIN.

You've deputed—whom did I hear you say?

LADY CASTLEJORDAN.

Sergeant Shuter.

MINCHIN.
Man or woman?

LADY CASTLEJORDAN.
From your point of view, woman, I suppose.

MINCHIN.
Why Sergeant?

LADY CASTLEJORDAN.
Late husband held that rank in Castlejordan's old regiment.

MINCHIN.
What duties does she—he—perform here?

LADY CASTLEJORDAN.
Teaches my boys boxing, fencing, athletics generally.

MINCHIN.
[*Groaning.*] Oh!

LADY CASTLEJORDAN.
A splendid fellow. At the same time, I should dearly like to have gone to Scrumleigh station to meet Noel.

MINCHIN.
You're detained here, I gather?

LADY CASTLEJORDAN.
Detained! I don't venture beyond the park now-a-days more than I can help. You know why, surely?

MINCHIN.
H'm! Well——

THE AMAZONS

LADY CASTLEJORDAN.

You know what they call me outside, at Great Overcote, and Little Overcote, and at Scrumleigh—ah, even in London!

MINCHIN.

Yes, yes.

LADY CASTLEJORDAN.

The Eccentric Lady Castlejordan. [*Scornfully.*] Eccentric!

MINCHIN.

My dear Lady Castlejordan, the truth is that I've presumed to call on you this morning in the hope that I may be permitted to modestly reason with you on this very subject.

LADY CASTLEJORDAN.

Again?

MINCHIN.

Once more.

LADY CASTLEJORDAN.

Sit down.

[*They sit; she on the camp-stool, he on the stump of a tree.*]

MINCHIN.

To begin with, it would be disingenuous to conceal from you that I do constantly hear very severe strictures passed upon your line of conduct.

LADY CASTLEJORDAN.

You've heard them for the last ten years, ever since my husband died.

MINCHIN.

But these strictures are more severe now than ever, and with some justice. When your children *were* children there was small harm in your playfully regarding them as boys and allowing them to romp and riot. But to-day here are three young women——

LADY CASTLEJORDAN.

No!

MINCHIN.

Three strapping young women——

LADY CASTLEJORDAN.

No!

MINCHIN.

I will repeat, I *do* repeat, three bouncing young women!

LADY CASTLEJORDAN.

Well, in detail, I admit my children are perhaps what you describe. But in disposition, in mind, in muscle, they are three fine, stalwart young fellows.

MINCHIN.

But Great Overcote, and Little Overcote, and Scrumleigh do not look upon them as——

LADY CASTLEJORDAN.

Are Great Overcote, and Little Overcote, and Scrumleigh competent judges of my bitter heart-burnings and disappointments? You knew Jack, my husband?

MINCHIN.

Ah, yes, indeed.

LADY CASTLEJORDAN.
What was he?
MINCHIN.
A gentle giant. A grand piece of muscular humanity. In frame, the Vikings must have been of the same pattern.
LADY CASTLEJORDAN.
And you remember me as I was twenty years ago?
MINCHIN.
[*Looking at her.*] I've no excuse for forgetting.
LADY CASTLEJORDAN.
I was a fit mate for my husband?
MINCHIN.
Perfect.
LADY CASTLEJORDAN.
Even in Jack's time I never scaled less than ten stone, and he could lift me as if I were a sawdust doll. Old friend——! Oh, old friend, what a son my son and Jack's ought to have been!
[*She goes to the gate and leans upon it, turning her back to* MINCHIN, *who has also risen.*]
MINCHIN.
But—but—but it didn't please Providence to send you a son.
LADY CASTLEJORDAN.
[*Beating the gate.*] Oh! Oh!
MINCHIN.
Come, come, do learn to view the matter resignedly!

LADY CASTLEJORDAN.

Girls, girls!

MINCHIN.

It's an old story now——

LADY CASTLEJORDAN.

Girls!

MINCHIN.

Why despise girls? Many people like girls. Bless my heart, *I* like girls!

LADY CASTLEJORDAN.

You can recall Noeline's arrival. I was sure she was going to be a boy—so was Jack. I knew it—so did Jack. The child was to have been christened Noel, Jack's second name.

MINCHIN.

Yes, I was up at the Hall that night, smoking with Castlejordan to keep him quiet.

LADY CASTLEJORDAN.

Poor dear, I remember his bending over me afterwards and whispering, "Damn it, Miriam, you've lost a whole season's hunting for nothing!" Then the second——

MINCHIN.

Lady Wilhelmina.

LADY CASTLEJORDAN.

Yes, Billy came next. Jack wouldn't speak to me for a couple of months after that, the only fall-out we ever had.

MINCHIN.

But your third, Lady Thomasin——

LADY CASTLEJORDAN.

Dearest Tommy! Oh, by that time Jack and I had agreed to regard anything that was born to us as a boy and to treat it accordingly, and for the rest of his life my husband taught our three children—there never was another—to ride, fish, shoot, swim, fence, fight, wrestle, throw, run, jump, until they were as hardy as Indians and their muscles burst the sleeves of their jackets. And, when Jack went, I continued their old training. Of course, I—I recognise my boys' little deficiencies, but I'm making the best of the great disappointment of my life, and I—well, call me the eccentric Lady Castlejordan! What do I care?

[*She sits, wiping her eyes.*

MINCHIN.

Ah, well, well! I've great sympathy. But I really do think that the time has arrived now——

LADY CASTLEJORDAN.

Now! Pardon me, but you can't know what you're talking about.

MINCHIN.

Eh?

LADY CASTLEJORDAN.

You haven't forgotten, have you, that the title went to my husband's brother in default of my being the mother of a—of a complete boy?

MINCHIN.

Of course I haven't.

LADY CASTLEJORDAN.

And that this man, the present Lord Castlejordan, a wizen creature without shoulders, has a son?

MINCHIN.

I know that.

LADY CASTLEJORDAN.

A son! And Lady Castlejordan a wisp of a woman with a mouth like a rabbit's! And they have a son!

MINCHIN.

Lord Litterly. He's at Oxford.

LADY CASTLEJORDAN.

He has just come down. And what do you think! That young man has carried everything before him at the University—everything!

MINCHIN.

Why, I heard he'd failed even to take a pass degree.

LADY CASTLEJORDAN.

Bother his degree! He was first string in the mile and quarter-mile against Cambridge at Queen's Club; he got his cricket blue and came within two of making his century at Lord's; and in Rugby football he was the best three-quarter back in the Oxford fifteen that's been known for the last five and twenty years. Oh! the torture of it!

MINCHIN.

Now, come, come! I don't see——!

LADY CASTLEJORDAN.

You don't see that this is the son Jack and I ought to have had! No! [*pacing to and fro.*] Heavens, if this young man had been sickly, stunted, freckled, weak, anæmic, red-eyed, narrow-chested——!

MINCHIN.

Hush, hush

LADY CASTLEJORDAN.

Or, better still, humpbacked, with one short leg, it might have made me a more contented, gentler woman! But, as it is——

MINCHIN.

Now, now!

LADY CASTLEJORDAN.

And you choose this moment for suggesting that I should look matters straight in the face and realise the melancholy maternal muddle I've made.

MINCHIN.

You know, I've had an idea for some time past—but, there, you're not on friendly terms with the present Lord Castlejordan and his family?

LADY CASTLEJORDAN.

[*Indignantly.*] Friendly terms!

MINCHIN.

Because it has often struck me that it might be a small consolation to you to know this young man——

LADY CASTLEJORDAN.

Never!

MINCHIN.

Tut, tut! You might grow to be fond of Lord Litterly.

LADY CASTLEJORDAN.

Fond of him! Fond of the youth that Nature— Nature, for whom I've done so much!—has taken from me and given to that insignificant little woman! No, never shall one of us exchange a word even with one of them! Never, I say! Never!

MINCHIN.

Oh, dear, oh, dear!

[LADY WILHELMINA BELTURBET *enters, below the hedge. She is a sweet-looking girl of nineteen, quite gentle and feminine. Her attire is a compromise between a boy's and a woman's; her " Norfolk " jacket reaches almost to her knees, and her lower limbs are encased in stout leathern gaiters. She carries a fishing-rod in its case and, across her shoulders, an ordinary wicker fishing-basket.*

WILHELMINA.

Why, it's Mr. Minchin! [*shaking hands with him warmly.*] Ah, mother dear! Mr. Minchin!

MINCHIN.

And, how are you, hey? Any sport?

WILHELMINA.

I'm on my way down. There's a little too much wind, I fancy. [*Slipping her basket from her shoulders.*] I've turned into the shelter here to tie a fly.

MINCHIN.
[*Opening the basket.*] Let me help you.
LADY CASTLEJORDAN.
What is Tommy doing this morning?
WILHELMINA.
Giving the grey mare a lesson over the hurdles.
MINCHIN.
H'm, dangerous work!
LADY CASTLEJORDAN.
[*Walking away.*] Please don't put such ideas into my boys' heads.
> [MINCHIN *and* WILHELMINA *sit side-by-side on the stump of the tree, he with her tackle-book in his hand.*]

MINCHIN.
[*Putting on his spectacles.*] Now then! What are your flies?
WILHELMINA.
Red Septembers and Mottled Spinners.
MINCHIN.
Ah, you're a knowing one. [*He ties the fly.*]
WILHELMINA.
Have you and mother been talking?
MINCHIN.
What d'ye think we have been doing—playing leap-frog?

WILHELMINA.

I mean talking about us gir—boys?

MINCHIN.

H'm! Pliers.

WILHELMINA.

[*Handing the pliers.*] I guess you have. Mr. Minchin, dear, mother isn't worried about us, is she—me particularly?

MINCHIN.

I can answer that. No, *she* isn't—*I* am. Silk.

WILHELMINA.

[*Giving the silk to him.*] I'm glad she's not worried. Because, do you know, I'm afraid I'm going to be a great sorrow to her.

MINCHIN.

You!

WILHELMINA.

I've a foreboding I shall turn out badly.

MINCHIN.

In what way?

WILHELMINA.

Oh, I'm getting worse every day, Mr. Minchin. I—I'm becoming so very effeminate. [*He looks at her for a moment then chuckles.*] Hush, hush!

MINCHIN.

Ho, ho! Scissors. Go on.

WILHELMINA.

It's nice to talk to you. Shall I tell you something very—well, rather—funny about Tommy and myself?

MINCHIN.

Do, if you ought to.

WILHELMINA.

I don't think I ought to.

MINCHIN.

[*Gravely.*] Well then, my dear, if you are at all uncertain about it perhaps it would be better——

WILHELMINA.

Yes, you're right.

MINCHIN.

Perhaps it would be better that you should tell me.

WILHELMINA.

Oh! Well, you know Tommy and I have been staying up at Drumdurris with little Lady Drum.

MINCHIN.

Have you?

WILHELMINA.

There was a very large house-party, men and women. [*He glances involuntarily at her gaiters.*] Oh, we always visit in our skirts, of course.

MINCHIN.

Yes, yes, yes.

WILHELMINA.

Well—you'll never guess!—Tommy had an offer of marriage.

MINCHIN.
[*Laughing.*] Ho, ho!

WILHELMINA.
Hush! You'll fall off.

MINCHIN.
That tom-boy too! Now, if such a thing had happened to *you*, I——

WILHELMINA.
Mr. Minchin!

MINCHIN.
Eh!

WILHELMINA.
It *did* happen to me also. [*Looking round.*] Mother! [LADY CASTLEJORDAN *reappears.*] I'm in the way, I expect.

MINCHIN.
[*Still laughing.*] No, no.

WILHELMINA.
My fly, please. Thank you.
[*She takes the fly from him; the hook runs into his finger.*

MINCHIN.
[*Yelling.*] Yah!

WILHELMINA.
You're hooked! [*Extracting the hook.*] I *am* sorry.
[*She gathers her tackle together and goes to the gate.*

LADY CASTLEJORDAN

[*To* MINCHIN.] I heard your laugh a long way off. What amuses you?

MINCHIN.

[*In pain.*] Got a hook in my finger.

LADY CASTLEJORDAN.

How good-humoured you are!

WILHELMINA.

Here's Tommy! [*Calling.*] Tom! Holloa—a—a!
  [*The call is returned and* LADY THOMASIN BELTURBET, *a bright, rosy, rather rough-mannered girl of eighteen, appears and leaps the gate. She is in man's riding-dress, smartly and perfectly turned-out from cap to boots.*

WILHELMINA.

Mr. Minchin has called to see us.

THOMASIN.

[*Shaking hands heartily with* MINCHIN.] Good man! How are you? [*Kissing* LADY CASTLEJORDAN.] Missed you at breakfast, mater. [*To* MINCHIN.] How's the old horse?

MINCHIN.

[*Shaking his head.*] Ah!

THOMASIN.

I thought he went rather gingerly on that near fore of his when you rode over in the summer. Look here, you come and have a spin with me round the park one morning; we'll give you a mount. What d'ye say?

MINCHIN.

[*Looking her up and down.*] My young friend, I'm afraid I could not ride with you while you are in such an attire as I now see you in—

LADY CASTLEJORDAN.

[*Interposing.*] Er—Mr. Minchin. Tommy, talk to your brother.

[THOMASIN *joins* WILHELMINA, *and they talk together.*

MINCHIN.

[*Advancing to* LADY CASTLEJORDAN, *speaking in an undertone.*] Lady Castlejordan, I—I must say it—I am a little shocked.

LADY CASTLEJORDAN.

I don't understand you.

MINCHIN.

Pardon me, is that a proper dress for a young woman to scamper about in?

LADY CASTLEJORDAN.

It is all a question of environment. The poor African in her solitary row of beads is as discreet as the best-dressed woman in town. I will not have my boys' unconsciousness disturbed.

MINCHIN.

I ought to tell you this. I hear that the Overcote

and Scrumleigh people spend the afternoons of their early-closing Wednesdays in hanging about the skirts of your park.

LADY CASTLEJORDAN.

Vulgar curiosity!

MINCHIN.

There, I wonder your park *has* skirts!

LADY CASTLEJORDAN.

I have built five lodges round Overcote Park, expressly to protect us from intruders; with the exception of one privileged old friend—yourself—no one enters the park but on my fortnightly Thursdays.

MINCHIN.

[*Glancing over his shoulder.*] And then——?

LADY CASTLEJORDAN.

Then my boys disguise themselves in petticoats. I think I may boast that no boys have sweeter frocks than my boys.

[WILHELMINA *and* THOMASIN *stroll away.*

MINCHIN.

[*Seeing that he is alone with* LADY CASTLEJORDAN.] H'm! one word more, Lady Castlejordan. Assuming, just for the sake of argument, that your boys are girls, may I ask what you'd do if they should ever be asked in marriage?

LADY CASTLEJORDAN.

[*Agitated.*] Ah! Oh, my dear Mr. Minchin!

MINCHIN.
[*Triumphantly.*] Aha!

LADY CASTLEJORDAN.

Do you know you've chanced on a supposition that has been a reality! While Willy and Tommy—well, Wilhelmina and Thomasin—were staying at Drumdurris Castle, two men fell in love with them!

MINCHIN.

And in the name of common-sense, why not?

LADY CASTLEJORDAN.

Men I call them! Insects! Merciful Powers, one was a Frenchman!

MINCHIN.

Well——!

LADY CASTLEJORDAN.

A creature who has doubtless shot a fox

MINCHIN.

The other?

LADY CASTLEJORDAN.

Little Lord Tweenwayes.

MINCHIN.

Tweenwayes! A fine race, the Fitzbrays.

LADY CASTLEJORDAN.

Fine!

MINCHIN.

Why Godefroy de Fitz Braye was one of Richard's Knights in the Crusade.

LADY CASTLEJORDAN.

No Fitzbray has ever stood higher than five feet five in his boots. They're a shrivelled, puny line. The present Lord Tweenwayes inherits the accumulated ailments of all his ancestors, and he presumes——!

THOMASIN *and* WILHELMINA *re-appear*.

MINCHIN.

Ssh!

LADY CASTLEJORDAN.

[*To* MINCHIN.] Walk up to the Hall with me; we shall just be in time to greet Lord Noel. I'll tell you about this business as we stroll along. [MINCHIN *opens the gate.*] My dear boys, don't come with us; it's so long since I've seen Mr. Minchin.

WILHELMINA.

Very well, mother dear.

THOMASIN.

All right, mater.

LADY CASTLEJORDAN.

[*As she and* MINCHIN *walk away.*] Isn't that Scrumleigh church chime? We shall be late.

[MINCHIN *and* LADY CASTLEJORDAN *disappear*. THOMASIN *sits on the tree-stump*.

THOMASIN.

So you think that, do you, Billy?

WILHELMINA.

Sure of it.

THOMASIN.

But why should the parson concern himself about us?

WILHELMINA.

He—he—thinks we're girls, you know, Tommy dear.

THOMASIN.

Well, we *ain't*, my dear William; so he's out of it.

WILHELMINA.

[*Approaching* THOMASIN *and kneeling beside her.*] Tom, don't you ever feel like a girl?

THOMASIN.

I! Well, I should hope not.

WILHELMINA.

But how do you know you don't? I'm sometimes afraid *I* do.

THOMASIN.

That's cos' you had measles too late in life and got your blood thin. You're a manly young chap enough, considerin'.

WILHELMINA.

Am I?

THOMASIN.

Of course, you're not to be compared with old Noel. He is the pick of our basket.

WILHELMINA.

Yes, he's very nice.

THOMASIN.

Nice! What silly words you use! Why, he's the best all-round sportsman our side of the county, even *I* own that. Nice! And he's a fellow that reads books too—*I* never could open a book. Nice! He—he—well he's just my notion of what a young Englishman ought to be. Hullo! What's that in the hollow of that tree?

WILHELMINA.

[*Quickly going across to the tree.*] Oh, can you see it?

THOMASIN.

See it?

WILHELMINA.

It must have slipped down; it's my guitar.
[*Drawing a guitar-case from the hollow of the tree.*

THOMASIN.

What the dooce——!

WILHELMINA.

Mother heard me playing in my room and stopped me. She says it's girlish.

THOMASIN.

Rubbish! The Troubadours always played guitars. Oh, I say, ain't I well-informed!

WILHELMINA.

[*Taking the guitar from its case.*] So I hid it here thinking I'd creep down to the Tangle sometimes and sing to myself.

THOMASIN.

Hard lines! Won't the mater let you play any thing?

WILHELMINA.

[*Tuning the guitar.*] She's promised to give me cornet.

THOMASIN.

Good business! Tune up, William. Anythin pretty—bar love-rot, you know.

WILHELMINA.

Ah, it's so damp!

[*As* WILHELMINA *is about to sing,* THOMASI *raises herself suddenly.*

THOMASIN.

Look out! Who's coming?

[WILHELMINA *hastily conceals the guitar an case below the tree.* LADY NOELINE BEI TURBET *and* SHUTER *are seen going toward the gate.* NOELINE *is a handsome, impe rious girl of twenty; she wears the ordinar travelling costume of a young lady.* SHUTE *is a good-looking woman of about thirty suggesting by her manner and dress a association with the army.* NOELINE *has set, serious look upon her face.* SHUTE *carries a travelling bag.*

WILHELMINA.

Noel!

THOMASIN.

[*Jumping up.*] Noel!

NOEL.

Boys!
[WILHELMINA *and* THOMASIN *grip* NOELINE'S *hands in manly fashion.*

NOELINE.

How are you?

THOMASIN.

How are you?

WILHELMINA.

How are you?

NOELINE.

How's the mother?

THOMASIN.

She was here just now with Mr. Minchin.

WILHELMINA.

They've gone up to the Hall, to meet you, I expect.

NOELINE.

I got out of the carriage at the East Lodge for the sake of a walk across the park. Sergeant!

SHUTER.

Yes, m'lord.

NOELINE.

Go on ahead. Tell my mother where I am. Don't stare at me like that, please.

SHUTER.

All right, m'lord. [*She goes off through the gate.*

WILHELMINA.

What is the Sergeant staring at? [*Looking into* NOELINE's *face.*] Oh!

THOMASIN.

[*Looking at* NOELINE.] By Jove, you don't look very fit!

NOELINE

[*Impatiently.*] Nonsense!

THOMASIN.

Glad to get back?

NOELINE.

[*Putting her hands on their shoulders.*] Glad! Rather!

THOMASIN.

Good man!

NOELINE.

[*Wearily.*] Let's sit down. Perhaps I am rather out of condition. London isn't Scotland.

[THOMASIN *hands* NOELINE *a cigarette case, from which she takes a cigarette, passing on the case to* WILHELMINA.

WILHELMINA.

[*Taking a cigarette.*] Thanks!

[*They light their cigarettes.*

THOMASIN.

You'll find these something good; I'm giving a new firm a leg-up.

NOELINE.

Boys, I had your letters. So you got into a little difficulty at Drumdurris?

THOMASIN.

Tweenwayes.

NOELINE.

Proposed, didn't he?

THOMASIN.

I should think he did!

NOELINE.

Nuisance, eh?

THOMASIN.

Horrid bore. Enough to turn any fellow against his holidays.

NOELINE.

What about you, Willy?

WILHELMINA.

[*Turning away slightly.*] A friend of Lord Tweenwayes.

THOMASIN.

André de Grival. You know, the usual thing—plenty of moustache and vivacity.

NOELINE.

Proposed?

WILHELMINA.

[*In a low voice.*] Oh, yes.

THOMASIN.

[*Strutting about.*] They behaved decently, I will say; they did go to Lady Drumdurris first, and Egidia in a great commotion wrote off to the mater.

WILHELMINA.

[*Sitting on the tree-stump beside* NOELINE.] But they couldn't wait for mother's reply.

NOELINE.

Caddish.

WILHELMINA.

Perhaps Monsieur de Grival is ignorant of our customs.

NOELINE.

Tweenwayes isn't.

WILHELMINA.

[*Putting her arm round* NOELINE'S *waist.*] You're vexed. It wasn't our fault. [*Kissing* NOELINE *furtively.*] You know, Tommy looked rather pretty up North.

NOELINE.

[*Looking into* WILHELMINA'S *face.*] I dare say.

[NOELINE *kisses* WILHELMINA.

WILHELMINA.

[*Taking* NOELINE'S *hand.*] Ah! [*Looking at* NOE-LINE'S *hand, suddenly*] Oh! Where's your ring?

NOELINE.

[*Snatching her hand away and concealing it.*] What?

WILHELMINA.

Your ring—the Belturbet ring!

NOELINE.

[*Agitated.*] It's in my case.

WILHELMINA.

Noeline! You know mother believes it never leaves your finger!

[THOMASIN *takes up the guitar, and sounds the strings.*

NOELINE.

[*Startled.*] What's that?

WILHELMINA.

My guitar.

NOELINE.

Sing to me, Willy—the train always upsets my nerves. Then we'll all walk home together.

[WILHELMINA *takes the guitar, and, leaning against the hollow tree, sings a pretty melody.* THOMASIN *sits on the gate.* NOELINE *remains on the tree-stump; as the song nears its close she sinks to the ground and, leaning her head on the stump, utters hysterical sounds.* WILHELMINA, *dropping her guitar, runs with* THOMASIN *to* NOELINE.

NOELINE.

Oh! Ha, ha, ha, ha! Oh dear, oh dear!

THOMASIN.

[*Raising her.*] Here! Hold up, old man!

WILHELMINA.

Noel! dear Noel!

NOELINE.

Oh, boys, boys, boys, I'm so upset.

THOMASIN.

What's amiss?

WILHELMINA.

Do tell us!

NOELINE.

Wait a second. I will tell you—I must tell somebody.

[*She walks up and down, composing herself. The others stand together and look on, wonderingly.*

THOMASIN.

[*To* WILHELMINA.] Eh!

WILHELMINA.

[*To* THOMASIN.] I can't think——

NOELINE.

I'm all right. I say, you fellows, I got into a bit of a mess the night before last—a scrape, a bother.

THOMASIN.

Did you?

WILHELMINA.

Oh!

THOMASIN.

How?

NOELINE.

You know, Mrs. Vipont and her husband went down into Surrey, to a political meeting he was to speak at, and as they couldn't catch the last train home they slept at Sir Henry Carholt's at Chilmere. I didn't go, for two reasons. Never-ending politics bore me, and then I—I wanted to profit by their absence to see London.

THOMASIN.

See London!

WILHELMINA.

Why, you have been seeing London for the last five weeks.

NOELINE.

Oh, yes, in my petticoats; shopping with Florence in the morning, the forlorn park in the afternoon, a cockney Exhibition in the evening. I wanted to view London from the same stand-point from which we've been brought up to see things here at Overcote.

THOMASIN.

Good man!

NOELINE.

Yes, that's it! I felt that if I could only parade the streets, as a man, at the hour when all the namby-pamby women of our class are being escorted here or there, lifted in and out of carriages, wrapped about in soft cloaks, half smothered by polite attentions—if I could only do this I should indeed be a man! I wanted to swagger along unnoticed, to fling away my half-burnt cigarette, to see it caught up still sparkling by a ragged urchin, to throw a coin to a crossing-sweeper, to be shoved and elbowed by a noisy crowd, ah, to be even sworn at—boys, I felt that if I could only do this I should be less like a girl than ever!

THOMASIN.

Oh, why wasn't I with you!

WILHELMINA.
And—and did you do it?

NOELINE.
[*After a little pause, gloomily.*] Yes, I did it. [*Sitting on the camp-stool.*] I did it.

THOMASIN.
[*Sitting, gleefully.*] Oh, ho, ho!

WILHELMINA.
[*Kneeling beside* NOEL.] You hadn't your dress clothes in town with you, Noel.

NOELINE.
No, but I was obliged to make a confidante of Dawkins, the woman who valeted me in Chesham Street, and she and I raked out a dress-suit of Bobby Vipont's. Bobby's in Switzerland, you know. He's seventeen and just my height, but everything I borrowed of him, except his white necktie, was a beastly fit. However, I was well hidden by his inverness cape, so it didn't matter a row of pins. Then I crammed my hair under a wig that had been left over from Lucy Vipont's birthday theatricals, and then—then Dawkins let me out.

THOMASIN.
[*Stamping her feet.*] What did you do? Where did you go to?

NOELINE.
[*Wearily.*] I did the West End. I—I didn't like it.

THE AMAZONS

I—I didn't care for anything I saw. I was tired—I was returning home. Then I got into this mess.

WILHELMINA.

[*Tremblingly.*] Oh, dear!

NOELINE.

I saw a man about to hit a girl. He'd got his arm back, his fist against his shoulder—he meant it. So did I! Boys, you know what I can do! Well, before you could have said "Jinks!" I'd slipped my big ring into Bobby Vipont's trouser pocket and I'd landed the monster—[*putting her fist under* WILHELMINA'S *chin*]—just here, Willy dear.

[THOMASIN *jumps up excitedly.*

WILHELMINA.

Noel!

NOELINE.

I've often knocked out Sergeant Shuter in the same way, but always with the gloves on. [*Rubbing her hand with aversion.*] Oh, you don't know what it's like to get home on a strange man's chin without the gloves on!

THOMASIN.

Did he go down?

NOELINE.

Down! [*Nodding, and staring at the ground in agitation.*] I see him there constantly. I tumble over him in my sleep. [*Going to* THOMASIN.] Oh, Tommy, Tommy!

THOMASIN.

Go on! don't stop.

NOELINE.

There was a crowd—men and women grew out of the pavement——

WILHELMINA.

Brutes!

NOELINE.

No, they were friendly. They called me "guv'nor." "Let him have it again, guv'nor," one person advised. An awful, unanimous desire seemed to possess them all to mind what they called my togs. My hat—Bobby Vipont's hat—went in a twinkling. Then terrible hands, hundreds of hands, I fancied, of all shapes and sizes, were laid on my cape. I wrenched myself free and broke away, hitting about like a woman then, right and left. And I ran. I ran till I fainted.

WILHELMINA.

You fainted! You!

NOELINE.

Why, don't men faint sometimes?

THOMASIN.

What became of you?

NOELINE.

When I came to I was lying on a sofa in a strange room and a young fellow was sitting, a little way off, watching me.

WILHELMINA.

Noel!

THOMASIN.

Noel!

NOELINE.
[*Awkwardly.*] Well?
THOMASIN.
Well? [*Impatiently.*] Well?
NOELINE.
I'd fallen almost into his arms, he explained. He'd taken me to his lodgings to get me round. He spoke as a gentleman speaks. He—he liked the look of me, he said.
THOMASIN.
[*Biting her lips.*] How did he convey you to his rooms? [NOELINE *shakes her head.*] Were you on a level with the street?
NOELINE.
No, first floor.
THOMASIN.
How did he get you upstairs?
NOELINE.
[*Rocking herself to and fro.*] That's just it!
THOMASIN.
[*Frowning.*] Think he guessed you—weren't the—usual sort of young man?
NOELINE.
I don't know what to think.
[WILHELMINA *bursts into tears.*
THOMASIN.
[*Hitting her boots with her crop, angrily.*] By Jove

this isn't a very nice accident to befall a young lady!

NOELINE.

[*Looking up.*] Tom!

THOMASIN.

Yes, you were sent to town as a young lady. [*Indignantly.*] A fellow's sister too! Well, well, well?

NOELINE.

He lent me a cap, expecting me, I suppose, to ask his name, but I snatched the cap from him and bolted down his stairs into the street. The dawn was just breaking when I found a cab. Dawkins put me to bed in a rage. When I got up I burnt the cap and gave Dawkins two pounds and a cigarette-holder. [*Wringing her hands.*] Oh! oh! [WILHELMINA *sobs.*

THOMASIN.

You shut up, William! [*To* NOELINE, *gloomily.*] After all, beyond the indignity and the humiliation of the thing, you're none the worse for the little outing——

NOELINE.

[*Holding out her hand.*] My ring! the Belturbet ring!

THOMASIN.

Eh!

NOELINE.

The big ring that has never left a Belturbet's hand for so many hundreds of years!

THOMASIN.

Not gone!

NOELINE.

It must have fallen out of the pocket of Bobby Vipont's silly trousers.

THOMASIN.

Jupiter! The mater's angry only about once a year; this'll be *it!* Look out! here they are!
> [WILHELMINA *hastily conceals the guitar and its case in the hollow of the tree.* NOELINE *draws on her gloves.* LADY CASTLEJORDAN, MINCHIN, *and* SHUTER *come through the gate.*

LADY CASTLEJORDAN.

[*Embracing* NOELINE.] My dear boy! [*Looking into* NOELINE'S *face, uneasily.*] Ah, London has taken that fine bronze tint out of your face. There's Mr. Minchin. [*Calling.*] Shuter! [SHUTER *advances.*

NOELINE.

[*Taking a letter from her pocket.*] Mrs. Vipont asked me to give you that, mother.
> [*She hands* LADY CASTLEJORDAN *the note, and joins* MINCHIN, WILHELMINA, *and* THOMASIN.

LADY CASTLEJORDAN.

[*To* SHUTER, *while opening the note.*] Sergeant!

SHUTER.

Yes, m'lady.

LADY CASTLEJORDAN.

Certainly, I do notice it. Lord Noel looks terribly flabby.

SHUTER.

I shall see what he does with the bar-bells to-night in the gymnasium.

LADY CASTLEJORDAN.

[*Reading the note to herself.*] Oh! "Dear Miriam. Please come to town at once to hear a statement from Clara Dawkins, my maid. Say nothing yet to Noeline as we may find the woman untruthful. Yours affectionately, Florence Vipont." Mercy! what has occurred? [*Calling.*] Mr. Minchin! [MINCHIN *approaches and* SHUTER *retires. The girls gather together.*] Old friend, will you take me to London this morning?

MINCHIN.

I?

LADY CASTLEJORDAN.

I must be protected from annoyance at Great Overcote and Scrumleigh. If you won't——

MINCHIN.

But I will!

LADY CASTLEJORDAN.

Oh, thank you! Not a word!
[*She goes hurriedly away through the gate.*

MINCHIN.

Lady Castlejordan——!
[*He follows her.* SHUTER *goes after them.*

THOMASIN.

[*Going to the gate.*] Anything wrong, Sergeant?

SHUTER.

[*Closing the gate.*] Hope not, m'lord.

[SHUTER *disappears.*

THOMASIN.

Why *is* the mater so taken up with Mr. Minchin to-day?

NOELINE.

It gives one breathing-time, at any rate. Come, boys, we'll go down to the bridge till lunch. Billy, bring the banjo.

[WILHELMINA *produces the guitar again.*

THOMASIN.

Yes, let's forget for a little while that you've lost Dad's ring. By Jove, its rippin' to be altogether again, ain't it!

NOELINE.

Ah, Tom, I wish we hadn't left home this summer any of us!

THOMASIN.

[*Slapping her on the back.*] Cheer up, old man!

NOELINE.

[*Rallying.*] I mean to. After lunch we'll have a pop at the partridges. Confound London! Hateful London!

[NOELINE *and* THOMASIN *go off below the hedge.*

WILHELMINA.

[*Running after them with the guitar.*] Wait for me, you fellows! Wait for me!

[*After a few moments,* ANDRÉ DE GRIVAL *emerges cautiously from the bush and undergrowth on the left below the hedge.* DE GRIVAL *is a good-looking, animated young Frenchman of the type of a Grévin caricature. He speaks fluently, but his pronunciation and inflections are, like his appearance and general demeanour, very French. Pieces of twig and bracken cling to his clothes and his necktie is disarranged.*

DE GRIVAL.

[*Looking about him.*] Where have we got to? Where is it? [*Wiping his brow.*] I am hot. [*Calling in an undertone.*] Tweenwayes, my dear fellow! Tweenwayes! [*The* EARL *of* TWEENWAYES *crawls out of the thicket, on his stomach, painfully.*] Tweenwayes, my friend, here we are sheltered. We may stand upright.

[LORD TWEENWAYES *rises. He is a short, thin, weak-looking man of about three-and-thirty, with a pale, emaciated face and red eyes. Although a most insignificant person, his bearing is full of affectation and his tone a haughty one. He is more disarranged and dishevelled than his companion, his clothes are covered with bracken, his hat and pocket are full of leaves, his knickerbockers are green and soiled at the knees, and, at one knee, there is a small rent.*

TWEENWAYES.

You don't think we've been observed?

DE GRIVAL.

Impossible. We crawl like alligators. Allow me.

[*Picking the bracken from* TWEENWAYES' *clothes and otherwise putting him in order.*] That was a good place at which to enter the park, between two lodges, not in sight of each. There you are.

TWEENWAYES.

Thank you; let me render you a similar service.

DE GRIVAL.

[*Turning his back to* TWEENWAYES.] My friend!
[TWEENWAYES *fastidiously removes one piece of bracken from* DE GRIVAL'S *coat.*

TWEENWAYES.

Yes, I certainly did discover the one weak spot in the fortification.

DE GRIVAL.

[*Removing the bracken from the front of his coat.*] Pardon me, *I* found it.

TWEENWAYES.

[*Politely, but annoyed.*] *I* found it.

DE GRIVAL

No, no, I found it.

TWEENWAYES.

[*Icily.*] I dare say you're right.
[*He replaces the piece of bracken on* DE GRIVAL'S *coat and moves away.*

DE GRIVAL.

Thank you. At all event, we are here. To fancy

I am once more near Wilhelmina, breathing the air she breathes, listening to the birds that sing to her, looking at———! [*To* TWEENWAYES, *who is sitting, emptying his pockets of leaves.*] My friend, you have scratched your nose.

TWEENWAYES.

No! [*Applying his handkerchief.*] Yes, it is so. Hah, this is characteristic of us! We have never hesitated to shed our blood freely for those on whom we have bestowed our affection.

DE GRIVAL.

We—us? You and me?

TWEENWAYES.

No, no, no—my race, my family. We have always been remarkable for our ardent passions. Our loves have made history, you know.

DE GRIVAL.

Lady Castlejordan's objection to you as a suitor for Lady Thomasin, have you heard it?

TWEENWAYES.

Heard it! She objects to my stature, my whole physical fabric, in fact. She is crazy on the subject of muscular development.

DE GRIVAL.

[*Feeling his muscles and hitting the air.*] Yes, yes. Ah! ah! [*Kicking vigorously.*] Ah!

TWEENWAYES.

[*Regarding* DE GRIVAL *disdainfully.*] We—*we* have

never been coarse, brawny men; always delicate, fragile, with transparent veins. Our women are especially interesting. An eminent surgeon once assured me that he could make out the osteological structure of any one of our women by placing her before a lighted candle and looking at her on the dark side. We——

DE GRIVAL.

And I am rejected because I am a Frenchman! Ah!

TWEENWAYES.

Well, frankly, with families who have made history, I can quite understand that that—but why pain you?

DE GRIVAL.

But I am English!

TWEENWAYES.

My dear De Grival!

DE GRIVAL.

English to my backbone! French by birth, yes. But so long educated in England, English in my appearance, manner, voice. I play your games, follow your sport. I speak the idiom of your language; I say "don'cher know!" frequently. I learn your proverbs—"a great many cooks spoil your broth, honesty is the best thing to do, a stick in time——" All of them, by heart. I say "damitall" in the smoking-room. And still I am French! Bah!

TWEENWAYES.

All I can say is I've known you some time and—well, we are judges of men.

DE GRIVAL.

My friend ! And we stick together in this affair ?

TWEENWAYES.

I will not leave this neighbourhood till I have personally renewed my proposal to Lady Thomasin. I am pleased to have your companionship.

DE GRIVAL.

But do we understand each other ? For example, if one of us was asked up to the Hall, that one would not march in and leave the other, his friend, on the outside ?

TWEENWAYES.

Speaking for myself, if I—well, dined at Overcote Hall without you, I should certainly make quite a point of alluding to you generously during the evening.

DE GRIVAL.

[*Enraged.*] Alluding ! Thank you very much ! Bah ! Never reckon your ducks—your chickens ! [*Snapping his fingers in* TWEENWAYES' *face.*] Don'cher know !

TWEENWAYES.

Monsieur de Grival !

DE GRIVAL.

[*Walking away.*] La, la, la !

TWEENWAYES.

[*Indignantly.*] Oh !
 [*They walk about angrily, then meet again.*

THE AMAZONS

After a display of irresolution, TWEEN-WAYES *removes a piece of the bracken from* DE GRIVAL'S *coat.*

DE GRIVAL.

[*Turning, conciliated.*] Ah! my friend!

TWEENWAYES.

[*Suddenly, in evident pain.*] Oh! Oh, dear me!

DE GRIVAL.

Tweenwayes, you have it again!

TWEENWAYES.

[*Writhing.*] No, no, the other was sciatica; this is cramp.

DE GRIVAL.

Cramp!

TWEENWAYES.

We have cramp. We have sciatica also, but every alternate generation has the cramp bias very clearly defined. Oh, dear, dear!

DE GRIVAL.

This from creeping through the underwood. What to do?

TWEENWAYES.

It will pass.

DE GRIVAL.

I suffer with you.

TWEENWAYES.

[*Rocking himself to and fro.*] Our cramp has made history. My mother quotes an old distich—
"Cold the wind and damp the day,
 Cramp shall seize the true Fitzbray!"

LORD LITTERLY *appears, above the hedge, and, seeing* TWEENWAYES *and* DE GRIVAL, *he looks cautiously over the gate. He is a handsome young man with the frame of an athlete and an air of indolence.*

LITTERLY.

[*To himself.*] I—I'll swear to that back! [*Aloud*] I say!

DE GRIVAL.

[*Turning.*] Eh? [*Going to the gate.*] My dear Barrington!

LITTERLY.

[*Opening the gate.*] André!
 [*They shake hands;* TWEENWAYES *groans.*

LITTERLY.

[*To* DE GRIVAL.] Who's your pal?

TWEENWAYES.

[*Looking round.*] How do you do, Litterly?

LITTERLY.

Why, Tweeny! what are you making that noise for?

DE GRIVAL.

The cramps.

LITTERLY.

[*Producing a little silver flask from his waistcoat pocket.*] Cramp! Take a pull. [TWEENWAYES *drinks.*] Why, we three haven't met since Lady Twombley's jolly dance that hot night in July. I say, what's this place?

DE GRIVAL.

Overcote Park.

LITTERLY.

No! Then it's my aunt's place!

TWEENWAYES.

Certainly it is.

DE GRIVAL.

Lady Castlejordan—your aunt? Ah, I see it!

LITTERLY.

The eccentric Lady Castlejordan they call her, poor lady. Are you visiting? [TWEENWAYES *and* DE GRIVAL *exchange looks.*] What's up?

DE GRIVAL.

Pardon me if I speak to Tweenwayes.
[DE GRIVAL *and* TWEENWAYES *consult together.*]

LITTERLY.

[*To himself.*] I say, suppose the young man I picked up—I mean, the young woman I picked up—turns out to be my—— [*With a prolonged whistle.*] Phew! I say!

DE GRIVAL.

[*To* LITTERLY.] No, we are not visiting. Are you?

LITTERLY.

I! My people and the Overcote Park people have been daggers-drawn for years.

TWEENWAYES.

You will, I am convinced, thank me, Litterly, for letting you know that no one is permitted to enter this park except on Lady Castlejordan's reception days.

LITTERLY.

[*Sitting lazily.*] So I believe. My cousins are rather uncommon in their rigs-out, I've heard.

TWEENWAYES.

Yes, yes, but—but here you are, my dear Litterly!

LITTERLY.

And here *you* are, my dear Tweeny.

TWEENWAYES.

Er—excuse me.
    [DE GRIVAL *and* TWEENWAYES *again consult.*
    LITTERLY *makes a cigarette calmly.*

DE GRIVAL.

My dear Barrington, we admit we have no rights here. The short of it is, we desire to meet Lady Wilhelmina Belturbet——

TWEENWAYES.

And Lady Thomasin——

DE GRIVAL.

Ladies we have had the joy of knowing at Drumdurris.

LITTERLY.

I say! Is that it?

DE GRIVAL.

To-day we discover the only way to enter this park without notice.

LITTERLY.

You think so? Well, no one saw me wriggle through a break in the fence, I swear.

DE GRIVAL.

Ah! We came through the fence also!

LITTERLY.

My dear aunt ought to have the park palings looked to.

DE GRIVAL.

[*Pointing to the left.*] Over there.

LITTERLY.

[*Pointing to the right.*] Over there.

TWEENWAYES.

[*Angrily.*] Pish!

DE GRIVAL.

Pardon me.

[TWEENWAYES *and* DE GRIVAL *again consult;* LITTERLY *chuckles.*

TWEENWAYES.

My dear Litterly, it is our deliberate intention to conceal ourselves in Overcote Park until we encounter these ladies. I need hardly tell you that any assistance you can render us, in the shape of leaving us to ourselves, we shall esteem highly.

LITTERLY.

[*Sitting on the grass, leaning lazily against the tree-stump.*] I say, I was about to make a similar suggestion to you, old chap. I'm going to hang about here too.

TWEENWAYES.

May I ask——?

LITTERLY.

Why not? I'm a little interested in a lady I've just seen entering the park. I've followed her from town, in point of fact, in the hope of getting a few words with her on the quiet. So you see, Tweeny, you can't have the field quite to yourself.

[TWEENWAYES *and* DE GRIVAL *consult together with great animation.*

TWEENWAYES.

I resent this! I resent it!

DE GRIVAL.

Damitall!

TWEENWAYES.

We—we don't brook obstacles.

DE GRIVAL,

A great many cooks! Damitall!

TWEENWAYES.

If this had occurred a few centuries ago we should have simply slain the fellow! [*After further muttered conversation they return to* LITTERLY.] My dear Barrington, it seems to us that as we are all trespassers here, and as our interests run on somewhat parallel lines, the best course we can adopt is to—is to——

DE GRIVAL.

Stick together.

LITTERLY.

Pals? I say, just as you like—don't put yourselves out.

DE GRIVAL.

Good! this is good! Union is strength! Don' cher know!

[*From the distance there comes the sound of the girls' voices, singing to the accompaniment of the guitar, and gradually drawing near.*

TWEENWAYES.

Hark!

DE GRIVAL.

Hark!

TWEENWAYES.

It's coming here. We'd better get out of sight.

DE GRIVAL.

Certainly. [*To* LITTERLY.] Barrington, you will be looked at! [DE GRIVAL *goes off quickly.*

TWEENWAYES.

Litterly! Litterly!

LITTERLY.

[*Preparing to rise.*] All right, old chap, I'm moving along.

TWEENWAYES.

Upon my word, Lord Litterly! [*Going down upon his hands and knees and crawling into the thicket, scowling at* LITTERLY.] Fool! fool! [*He disappears.*

LITTERLY.

[*Rising slowly and listening.*] Girls' voices. Girls.
    [*He walks off after* DE GRIVAL. *Then* NOELINE, WILHELMINA, *and* THOMASIN *come along singing.*

THOMASIN.

[*Near the gate, speaking to* WILHELMINA.] Look out, Billy! Here's the Sergeant.
    [*They cease singing.* WILHELMINA *hurriedly returns the guitar to its hiding-place.* THOMASIN *stands shielding* WILHELMINA *as* SHUTER *approaches.*

SHUTER.

[*From the other side of the gate.*] My lady would like to see you up at the Hall directly; she wants to say good-bye.

NOELINE.

Good-bye?

WILHELMINA.

Good-bye?

THOMASIN.

Good-bye?

SHUTER.

M'lady's just off to town.

NOELINE.

To town?

THOMASIN.

What for?

WILHELMINA.

Going to London?

NOELINE.

Mother has been sent for by the lawyers, perhaps.

WILHELMINA.

She's going to see the dentist, very likely.

THOMASIN.

Hairdresser, *I* think. Mater's hair is coming out in sackfuls.

WILHELMINA.

Dressmaker, I believe.

THOMASIN.

Or bootmaker; mater hasn't got a decent shoe to her back—I mean——

NOELINE.

Don't stand here guessing. Come on, boys.

[SHUTER *opens the gate.* THOMASIN *shoulders the campstool;* WILHELMINA *picks up her rod and basket. The three girls disappear, and* SHUTER *follows. Then* DE GRIVAL *returns excitedly.*

54 THE AMAZONS

DE GRIVAL.

[*To his companions.*] Ssst! Ssst! [TWEENWAYES *crawls from out the thicket.* LITTERLY *re-enters leisurely.*] Wilhelmina! I have seen Wilhelmina!

TWEENWAYES.

Hush! Thomasin! I have heard Thomasin!

LITTERLY.

[*To himself.*] My cousin! The boy I picked up—well, the girl I picked up—my cousin!

DE GRIVAL.

[*To* TWEENWAYES.] Did you hear? Lady Castlejordan goes to London! Do you understand that?

TWEENWAYES.

Dash it, do you think I'm obtuse?

DE GRIVAL.

What fortune! The mother goes! We see them, talk with them, walk with them! La, la, la! Love laughs at blacksmiths! Don' cher know!
  [*He dances about fantastically.* LITTERLY *sits thoughtfully. The girls are heard singing again, their voices gradually becoming more distant.*

DE GRIVAL.

[*Rushing to the gate.*] Again!
  [LITTERLY *rises on hearing the singing, and running to the gate, climbs on to the middle bar and looks off.*

TWEENWAYES.
You'll be seen by the maid! [*Going down on his hands and knees and crawling to the gate*] Fool! fool! [*He puts his head under the lower bar to watch the girls. The girls are still singing in the distance.*

END OF THE FIRST ACT.

THE SECOND ACT

The scene is the same as in the preceding Act. FITTON, *the gamekeeper, an old man, is sitting and smoking a clay pipe, while a dog lies near him.*

THOMASIN.
[*Calling in the distance.*] Fitton! Fitton!

FITTON.
[*Rising and putting his pipe away.*] 'Ere I be, m'lord.

He opens the gate. THOMASIN *enters, followed shortly by* WILHELMINA *and after a brief interval by* NOELINE. *The three girls are in clothes fashioned after the style of a man's shooting suit—corduroy coats and waistcoats, tweed knickerbockers, shoes and gaiters, everything very smart and natty. They carry their guns.*

THOMASIN.
Kept you waiting, Fitton?

FITTON.
Not you, m'lord.

WILHELMINA.

Good afternoon, Jo.

FITTON.

Arternoon, m'lord.

NOELINE.

Well, Jo, how are you?

FITTON.

Glad to see ye back agin, m'lord.

THOMASIN.

What's the programme?

FITTON.

[*To Noel.*] I thought we'd try the plantations furst, m'lord.

NOELINE.

That'll do. Get us back to tea—what time, Billy?

WILHELMINA.

Youatt will be here with the tea-basket at a quarter to four.

FITTON.

We'll work up toward Silverthorn Coppice arter tea; birds be feedin' theer about sunset.

NOELINE.

Get along, boys.

[THOMASIN, WILHELMINA, *and* NOELINE *go off below the hedge,* FITTON *following with the dog. After a pause,* DE GRIVAL *comes hastily behind the hedge, and clambers over the gate.*

DE GRIVAL.

[*Calling.*] Tweenwayes ! my friend !
[TWEENWAYES *runs up, attempts to climb the gate, falls over, and is caught by* DE GRIVAL.

TWEENWAYES.

[*Sitting, much agitated.*] Confound the thing !

DE GRIVAL.

[*Looking over the gate, then joining* TWEENWAYES.] They have stopped running.

TWEENWAYES.

An ancestor of mine, Ughtred Fitz Bray, called "the Uncomely," brought inevitable destruction—so the legend goes—on those whom he cursed in anger. Curse these cows !

DE GRIVAL.

First we come face to face with the deer—we leave them. Then we come face to face with the bulls—we leave them. Then——

TWEENWAYES.

Oh, it's a beastly park ! This is the only decent bit of retirement.

DE GRIVAL.

[*Walking about impatiently.*] But here we do not meet the ladies ; here we shall never meet the ladies.

TWEENWAYES.

Pardon me, if the ladies are out they must come here to get away from the cows.

DE GRIVAL.

One thing we may congratulate ourselves. We have lost Barrington.

TWEENWAYES.

Ah, yes, we're rid of Litterly. [*Pacing up and down angrily.*] We soon tired *him* out.

DE GRIVAL.

I am glad. Two are company, three is too much. Don' cher know!

TWEENWAYES.

His society had already become intolerable to me. The boundless self-sufficiency of the man! Once, when he trod on my foot, I was within an ace of cursing him. I doubt his breeding too. The idea of his tracking a pretty face from town in this way! The circumstance of his turning out to be the lady's cousin doesn't excuse him; I believe he simply met her in a shop and followed her about like a snobby cad. It's an accursed impropriety. Heavens, is chivalry extinct? What—eh?

DE GRIVAL.

[*With a little groan.*] Tweenwayes, my friend, I am hungry.

TWEENWAYES.

Hungry! I feel like a disused vault.

DE GRIVAL.

Bah! It is an hour past my lunch.

TWEENWAYES.

You forget, you did breakfast, I didn't. I may tell you, we—we never breakfast.

DE GRIVAL.

[*Turning away.*] We, we, we!

TWEENWAYES.

If we miss our midday meal we have acute sinking of the stomach. My aunt quotes a quaint old quatrain—
"In the battle, let the strongest,
Who the bold Fitzbrays would scatter,
Seek out those who've been the longest
Parted from their cup and platter."
We——

DE GRIVAL.

My friend, I am tired of your we—we!

TWEENWAYES.

Monsieur de Grival!

DE GRIVAL.

La, la, la!

TWEENWAYES.

[*Furiously.*] Leave the park, leave the park!

DE GRIVAL.

[*Facing* TWEENWAYES, *excitedly.*] Possession is nine points of your law!

TWEENWAYES.

You forget yourself!

DE GRIVAL.

First come, first serve! [*contemptuously waving his hand under* TWEENWAYES' *nose.*] Don' cher know.

TWEENWAYES.

Ah!
[*They separate and walk about, then they stand apart, eyeing each other furtively.*

DE GRIVAL.

[*Advancing to* TWEENWAYES *hesitatingly.*] Pardon me.

TWEENWAYES.

[*To himself, struggling inwardly.*] Can I?
[TWEENWAYES *at length offers* DE GRIVAL *two fingers.*

DE GRIVAL.

[*Dubiously.*] My friend!
[LITTERLY *strolls along, below the hedge, smoking.* TWEENWAYES *and* DE GRIVAL *exchange looks of disgust.*

LITTERLY.

[*Sitting.*] Seen anybody?

DE GRIVAL.

Not we. What have you been doing, my dear Barrington?

LITTERLY.

Having a bit of lunch.

TWEENWAYES.

[*Advancing eagerly.*] Where, where, where?

LITTERLY.

[*Pointing over his shoulder.*] Found a most delightful rural inn close by—" The Checkers," at Little Overcote. I say, if you two would like to patronise it, I'll keep watch here for the ladies willingly.

TWEENWAYES.

Accept my thanks, but I prefer not to quit my post. We—we never——

DE GRIVAL.

Nor I too. I will not leave the park till I have seen Wilhelmina.

LITTERLY.

All right; you please yourselves.
 [TWEENWAYES *and* DE GRIVAL *walk about aimlessly.*

TWEENWAYES.

[*After a pause.*] What did they give you to eat?

LITTERLY.

Grilled bacon——

TWEENWAYES *and* DE GRIVAL.

Oh!
 [*They go off quickly, below the hedge,* TWEEN-
 WAYES *dropping on to his hands and knees
 and disappearing into the thicket.*

LITTERLY.

[*Chuckling.*] Ha, ha, ha! Ten pounds to a button they follow that path to the left instead of crossing the brook. I say! Keep to the right, you fellows——!
  [*He goes after* DE GRIVAL. *Directly he has disappeared* NOELINE *enters, below the hedge, leaning on* THOMASIN'S *arm.*

THOMASIN.

How did you manage to come such a cropper?

NOELINE.

Put my foot in a rabbit-hole.

THOMASIN.

What's your ankle like now?

NOELINE.

Better. But my wrist—I can't hold my gun.
  [*She sits on the tree-stump.*

THOMASIN.

[*Placing her gun against the tree.*] Poor old man!

NOELINE.

[*Holding her wrist.*] Don't mind me; go after Billy and Fitton.

THOMASIN.

Sha'n't.

NOELINE.

I'll pick you up in a few minutes. [*Moving her hand*] It's easier already.
  [*There is a sound of a shot in the distance.*

NOELINE.
That's Billy's gun.
THOMASIN.
[*To herself.*] Oh, the sneak!
[THOMASIN *runs off unnoticed by* NOELINE.
LITTERLY *reappears.*

LITTERLY.
[*Seeing* NOELINE *and speaking to himself.*] My boy—my girl—my cousin!
[*He rustles the fallen leaves with his stick.*

NOELINE.
[*Without turning.*] Oh, do go! I promise to join you in five minutes.

LITTERLY.
[*Approaching her.*] Eh?

NOELINE.
[*Rising, with a gasp, and facing him.*] Sir!

LITTERLY.
You—you weren't speaking to me?

NOELINE.
I—I—I don't know you.

LITTERLY.
My name is Litterly—Lord Litterly.

NOELINE.
[*Staring at him wildly.*] You—Lord Litterly!

LITTERLY.

You must be one of the Ladies Belturbet. Lady———?

NOELINE.

Noeline.

LITTERLY.

I say, we're related.

NOELINE.

[*Nodding, still unable to remove her eyes from him.*] Yes.

LITTERLY.

There's no love lost between your branch of the family and mine. I suppose we don't shake hands?

NOELINE.

Certainly not.

LITTERLY.

No. I thought I'd raise the point.

NOELINE.

[*Pulling herself together.*] I—I am sorry to have to tell you—you are trespassing here.

LITTERLY.

Yes, yes, I suppose I am. [*Strolling up to the gate.*] I say, pretty park. Pardon me—my bootlace.
[*He puts his foot on the bar of the gate and ties his bootlace.*]

NOELINE.

[*To herself, clenching her hands.*] How can he have found out I am the young fellow he carried home to

E

his lodgings! The cad, to take advantage of it like this! My cousin too! The cad! Oh! [*Taking up her gun as if to go, then turning to* LITTERLY, *haughtily.*] I don't assume that you are ignorant of the way in which my mother has trained her children.

LITTERLY.

No, no, don't assume I'm ignorant.

NOELINE.

Nor do I think it worth while to defend—and to you!—the lives we live here. I must say, however, that I can see only one possible disadvantage attached to our mode of existence.

LITTERLY.

Tailor's bills?

NOELINE.

[*Going.*] I mean the necessity for regarding uninvited guests as unmannerly intruders.

LITTERLY.

Lady Noeline! Do stay a moment. I fagged down here thinking I was perhaps going to render somebody a trifling service.

NOELINE.

A service?

LITTERLY.

Just sit down a minute. Now do! [*Looking about.*] Take a—[*Pointing to the tree-stump.*] Take a stump. Do!

[*After a moment's irresolution, she returns and sits, defiantly nursing her gun.*

THE AMAZONS 67

LITTERLY.

[*Standing near her.*] Thanks. This is how it comes about——

NOELINE.

Do you mind going further off?

LITTERLY.

Not a bit. [*Looking round.*] Ah, the ottoman!
[*He sits on the gate. During the scene which follows he watches her closely but playfully, telling his story with great relish. She listens intently, with her back turned to him.*

NOELINE.

[*To herself, after glancing at him.*] The—utter—cad!

LITTERLY.

Lady Noeline, this is my little story. The night before last, as I was walking home from my club, a young gentleman, who had evidently got himself into some bother, ran straight into my arms and, having arrived there, stayed there. The poor young chap had fainted.

NOELINE.

Well——?

LITTERLY.

I was puzzled what the dooce to do. He seemed a nice young fellow. I say, what would you have done?

NOELINE.

I—I really don't know.

LITTERLY.

I'll tell you what I did in the end. There was no one about; I couldn't drop him into the mud or hand him over to the police—could I?

NOELINE.

Oh, no, you couldn't have done that!

LITTERLY.

No. I hailed a cab and took him off to my lodgings. He did seem such a nice young fellow.

NOELINE.

[*Writhing.*] Will you please go on with your story, if you must tell it me?

LITTERLY.

Certainly. Where was I? Oh yes—he *did* seem such a nice young fellow.

NOELINE.

I don't want to hear what sort of young fellow he appeared to be!

LITTERLY.

No, no, it doesn't really belong to the story. Well, I took him home and carefully deposited him on the sofa.

NOELINE.

[*To herself.*] Cad!

LITTERLY.

He was a good-looking Johnnie.

NOELINE.

Lord Litterly——!

LITTERLY.

I beg pardon—that's nothing to do with it. By-and-bye he came round. But I didn't succeed in making much of him. I fancied he was off his head, which reminded me that he'd lost his topper. So I offered to lend him a cap. I say, you should have seen the way he grabbed at it! Then he bolted down my stairs and, in point of fact, hooked it. [*Getting off the gate*] Now this *is* the story—it was a new cap. He hadn't even said thanks for the loan of it, and that riled me. So down I went after him and followed his cab to a house in Chesham Street. Ha, ha! What d'ye think of that?

NOELINE.

I—I fail to see the smallest necessity for you to—to have followed this—person about.

LITTERLY.

It was a brand-new cap.

NOELINE.

You might have known it would be returned—— [*To herself, recollecting.*] Oh!

LITTERLY.

Well, I did follow him, and there it is. Now, notwithstanding his bad form, he still struck me as being a nice young fellow.

NOELINE.

[*Rising.*] I can*not*—

LITTERLY.

Yes, now I think of it, that *does* belong to the story. [*Looking at her fixedly.*] He seemed such a nice young fellow that, somehow, I couldn't drive him out of my head, and next day I found myself hanging about that house in Chesham Street hesitating whether I'd go and bang away at his door.

NOELINE.

[*With her eyes averted.*] What for?

LITTERLY.

[*Still watching her intently.*] What for? Well—there was the cap.

NOELINE.

A paltry cap!

LITTERLY.

A *new* paltry cap. However, I didn't knock—I'm such a slow man. But early this morning I was in Chesham Street again, and while I was lolling against a lamp-post, out *you* came with another lady, and got into a luggage-brougham. I say, it was an awful job, chasing that brougham to Paddington station——

NOELINE.

The idea of your doing such a thing! What an intolerable liberty! [*She goes indignantly up to the gate, where she stands with her back to him.*] The mere idea of it! Oh!

LITTERLY.

[*To himself, watching her admiringly.*] I say, she's glorious! And to think that I carried *that* up seven-

and-twenty stairs! She hates me for it—but I've counted 'em! [*To her.*] Lady Noeline, there's a look in your shoulders that tells me you'd like me to explain why I followed you. [*She quickly changes her position, still averting her face.*] The fact is, I saw a strong likeness in you to that Johnnie, the sort of likeness a big sister might bear to a cub of a brother. And I felt an uncontrollable desire to have a jaw with you. [*Leaning against the trunk of the tree.*] You know I didn't find out till an hour ago that we're cousins.

NOELINE.

[*Eyeing him furtively.*] However marked the resemblance may be between me and the individual you picked up, you will find it difficult to justify your pursuing a woman in this way. Wanting "a jaw" doesn't quite do it!

LITTERLY.

[*Seriously.*] Lady Noeline, I thought if I could get five minutes' chat with the girl who bears such a strong resemblance to that nice young fellow, I could advise her to keep an eye on—shall we call him her brother?—in future. I thought I might, through her, save that nice young chap from some day falling into another difficulty when perhaps there would be no *me* to pick him up carefully and take him out of harm's way. I thought perhaps I might convince him, through her, that the West End of London—the Worst End of London—at night-time is not a locality where even a self-respecting cat may trust himself. And this, Lady Noeline, is how I come to trespass in Overcote Park.

NOELINE.

[*To herself, in a low voice.*] He's not—such a cad. It's positively delicate of him to avoid referring to me point-blank. He can't be an out-and-out cad. [*To* LITTERLY, *her tone slightly altered.*] I—I understand now the service you wished to render, and I—I—I quite appreciate your intentions.

LITTERLY.

There's one other small matter; [*taking a ring from his waistcoat pocket*] that Johnnie left his ring on my hearthrug.

NOELINE.

Eh? Oh!

LITTERLY.

[*Examining the ring.*] Rummy old thing it seems to be.

> [*They stand together for a time not speaking, he handling the ring, amused, she eagerly but irresolutely eyeing it. Then he offers it to her silently and she slips it hastily into her pocket.*

NOELINE.

[*Putting her gun under her arm.*] You—you have taken a great deal of trouble——

LITTERLY.

Pooh! not worth talking about.

NOELINE.

Er—er—good afternoon. [*As she is going she*

meets FITTON, *and says to him*] Oh! you've come back for me, I suppose?

FITTON.

[*Eyeing* LITTERLY *and speaking to* NOELINE.] Beg pardon, m'lord; for interruptin'——
                    [LITTERLY *strolls away.*

NOELINE.

Er—Fitton, this is my cousin, Lord Litterly. A—a sort of accident has brought him into the park——

FITTON.

Accidents will 'appen, m'lord.

NOELINE.

My mother would be extremely angry if she knew. Jo, I don't think it's necessary to tell her about it. [*Impatiently.*] Oh, come on!

FITTON.

[*Detaining her.*] M'lord it beaint no good goin' arter t'others.

NOELINE.

What do you mean?

FITTON.

Lord William and Lord Thomas and me worked round from plantations to Hexly Bottom, and just as we was all pickin' our way 'cross th' brook, darn me if we didn't fall over two other gentlemen!

NOELINE.

Jo!

FITTON.

[*Rubbing his head.*] Odd rabbit it if we get another shot this arternoon!

NOELINE.

Why, where are Lord Willy and Lord Tommy?

FITTON.

Walkin' about wi' 'un, talkin' to 'un——

NOELINE.

[*Going to* LITTERLY *and speaking hotly.*] Do you know anything of this? The keeper says there are two men in the park with my brothers—my sisters!

LITTERLY.

Lord Tweenwayes and André de Grival.

NOELINE.

Oh!

LITTERLY.

They're with me—I'm with them—we're with each other.

NOELINE.

[*Facing him indignantly.*] You—you—you are precisely what I first thought you! [*She runs off.*

LITTERLY.

[*Following her.*] No, I'm not! Lady Noeline, what is it you thought me? I say——!

[*Disappears after her.*

FITTON.

[*Calling after them.*] You won't find 'em theer, I ell 'ee! They be away by Hexly Bottom! [*Turning way.*] Oh, dang it! Boys will be boys, they do say —lord, seems to me boys will be gels here in Overcote Park!

WILHELMINA *enters below hedge, followed by* DE GRIVAL.

WILHELMINA.

[*To* FITTON, *in a frightened tone.*] Jo, have you seen Lord Noel?

FITTON.

[*Pointing off.*] He's gone arter ye, m'lord, wi'another gentleman—Lord Latterby or some sich.

WILHELMINA.

[*To* DE GRIVAL.] Lord Litterly is with Noel. [*Partly to herself.*] Then Noel can't be so very angry with me and Tommy. [*Taking* FITTON *aside.*] Fitton—
      [WILHELMINA *gives instructions to* FITTON.
      THOMASIN *enters from above the hedge followed by* TWEENWAYES.

THOMASIN.

[*Leaning on the gate.*] Billy, Lord Tweenwayes and Monsieur De GRIVAL will take tea with us, of course. Don't forget, extra cups and saucers to come down from the house!

WILHELMINA.

I am ordering them now. [*Stamping her foot.*] You're making me do everything!

THOMASIN.

[*To* TWEENWAYES.] Come on, Tweenwayes. You must see our new Hereford bulls. [*She goes off.*

TWEENWAYES.

[*Hesitating at the gate—to himself.*] She *will* take me to the cattle! [*To* DE GRIVAL.] Get away from here as soon as you can—I'm coming back.

DE GRIVAL.

My friend, you must find some other place to make your love in—I want it.

THOMASIN.

[*In the distance.*] Tweenwayes!

TWEENWAYES.

Oh! [*Going—and saying to himself as he looks at* DE GRIVAL *indignantly.*] Insolent! Insolent!

[*He follows* THOMASIN.

FITTON.

[*To* WILHELMINA.] Don't 'ee be afeared, m'lord. I'll make it all right wi' Youatt. [*To himself.*] Youatt don't get no more game out o' me for his sister in Lunnon if he can't keep his mouth shut.

[FITTON *disappears;* WILHELMINA *sits on the tree-stump, and* DE GRIVAL *comes down and kneels by her side.*

WILHELMINA.

Monsieur de Grival!

DE GRIVAL.

[*With great fervour.*] Wilhelmina! Ah, you are
orable! You are enchanting! You are perfect!
, you are—you are—you are pretty good!

WILHELMINA.

[*With her handkerchief to her eyes.*] Oh, it isn't kind
you to be so persistent!

DE GRIVAL.

Faint heart never won a fair-haired young lady!
n'cher know!

WILHELMINA.

But nothing, nothing would ever reconcile my
ther to your nationality.
  [*She shifts her gun from one knee to another;
    the muzzle chancing to point towards* DE
    GRIVAL.

DE GRIVAL.

My nationality! Absurd trifle! [*Disconcerted by
 presence of the gun.*] French by birth, yes. But Eng-
h in my appearance— English in my—— [*Rising,
ing behind* WILHELMINA, *and kneeling on her left.*]
ench by birth, yes. But English in my appearance,
anner, voice. Do I not play your games, your golf,
ur cricket ?—no, not your cricket ! Do I not speak
ur proverbs—" Set a thief to catch himself "—all of
em ? Do I not say " Damitall " in the smoking-
om——?

WILHELMINA.

Oh!

78   THE AMAZONS

DE GRIVAL.

No, I do not!

WILHELMINA.

You don't fully realise the extent of my mother's prejudice. According to her notion, a Frenchman can never be a thorough sportsman—

DE GRIVAL.

How wrong the notion! For example, let her once see me riding in the paper-chase. In the paper-chase, nine out of ten, I am always—always—in at the decease. I——

WILHELMINA.

I assure you that would weigh very lightly with my mother. [*Inadvertently she again shifts her gun so that it points at* DE GRIVAL'S *face.*] Oh, please, please give up hoping, Monsieur de Grival!

DE GRIVAL.

[*Again uncomfortable.*] Give up hoping! Give up— do you imagine—it is not poss——! [*Rising, he takes the gun from* WILHELMINA *and places it against the opposite tree.*] Pardon me. Never play with edged guns.

TWEENWAYES *enters quickly, followed by* THOMASIN. TWEENWAYES *opens the gate to let* THOMASIN *through, then closes it sharply and looks off.*

THOMASIN.

[*Coming down to* WILHELMINA]. Tweenwayes has been admiring our Herefords.

DE GRIVAL.

[*Knowingly.*] Has he? Ha, ha! I laugh!

TWEENWAYES.

[*Eyeing* DE GRIVAL *witheringly.*] I should much like Monsieur de Grival to examine the Hereford bulls.

DE GRIVAL.

[*Startled.*] Ah!

TWEENWAYES.

Perhaps Lady Wilhelmina!

WILHELMINA.

[*Going up to the gate.*] With pleasure. Monsieur de Grival——?

DE GRIVAL.

[*Uncomfortably.*] You honour me. [TWEENWAYES *opens the gate;* WILHELMINA *passes through.* DE GRIVAL *follows, then returns for the gun, saying to himself.*] In case. Prevention is better than being run after. [*To* TWEENWAYES, *insultingly, in passing him.*] Don'cher know!

TWEENWAYES.

[*Falling back.*] Ah! [WILHELMINA *goes off followed by* DE GRIVAL, *then* TWEENWAYES *climbs on to the gate, looking after them.*] Insolent! May they toss him like a common coin! Insolent!

[*He joins* THOMASIN *who is sitting on the stump, lighting a cigarette.*

THOMASIN.

[*Offering him her cigarette case.*] Smoke?

TWEENWAYES.
Thank you, no. We Fitzbrays do not smoke.

THOMASIN.
How a man can exist without it puzzles me.

TWEENWAYES.
We drink.

THOMASIN.
No! What, too much?

TWEENWAYES.
Alternate generations have the drink bias very clearly defined.

THOMASIN.
Where do you come in?

TWEENWAYES.
The predilection skips me. My father was called "Three-bottle Tweenwayes." But, in one way and another, he made a good deal of history in his time.

THOMASIN.
It must be a bad business to be a tippling Tweenwayes.

TWEENWAYES.
[*Walking away a little annoyed.*] Pardon me, we don't think so.

THOMASIN.
[*Following him.*] I say, Tweenwayes, I'm still thinking over what you've told me about this fellow,

Litterly, following my brother Noel from town and intruding himself here——

TWEENWAYES.

Pray dismiss that topic for the moment. [*Formally.*] Lady Thomasin, for the third time—I love you.

THOMASIN.

Oh, shut up, Tweeny!

TWEENWAYES.

We—we are always listened to.

THOMASIN.

[*Stamping her foot.*] Oh!
 [*She goes to the gate and leans upon it, with her back towards him.*

TWEENWAYES.

[*Walking to and fro.*] Lady Thomasin, it would be an easy task to descant on your beauty, your amiability. But, when I express my conviction that my family would regard our engagement with favour, it seems to me I say everything. Heavens, what a test to apply to a woman, and yet you emerge from the ordeal unscathed! The Fitzbray legend runs—[*To himself.*] Dash it! how does it run——?

THOMASIN.

[*To herself.*] Of course, Tweeny's right—the fellow must have been simply attracted by Noel's face. Confound him!

F

TWEENWAYES.

I've got it—
"Search the south and sweep the north,
Scour the east and spoil the west,
Speed your emissaries forth
To the fairest and the best.
Storm the cities' topmost heights,
Steal about the countryside—
When ev'ry grace in one unites
You will have found a Fitzbray's bride!"

THOMASIN.

[*To herself.*] The mater's often told us that those other Belturbets are outsiders——!

TWEENWAYES.

[*Resuming his march.*] On the subject of my claims upon your esteem my own mouth is necessarily closed. But there's a sentence in a letter I received yesterday from my sister, Lady Clandunphie—[*searching for a letter*]—which perhaps—you—ought to—[*finding it*] —Ah!
    [*He produces a letter, and a large reading-glass in a case.*

THOMASIN.

[*Eyeing the reading-glass.*] Hullo, what's that machine?

TWEENWAYES.

We have no sight to speak of. [*Reading.*] "One thing, dearest Galfred, I would urge upon you, to guide you in your quest of a woman fitted to figure with you in history's page, and that is the constant reflection that you preserve in your own person all that is noblest and best of the mediæval spirit." [*Advancing to* THOMASIN.] Lady Thomasin——

THOMASIN.

Look here, old man, we're delighted to see you here to tea while the mater's away, to show you the Herefords and all that—but drop the rest. Even if I were inclined to turn myself into a girl, which I *ain't*, the mater wouldn't hear of anybody but a man with a chest that 'ud take you the best part of the afternoon to drive round.

TWEENWAYES.

[*Putting away the letter and glass.*] Can it be possible! However, we have never hesitated at self-sacrifice. If you could suggest any easy means of muscular development——

THOMASIN.

By Jove! Tweeny, if you *did* want to show what you're made of——!

TWEENWAYES.

Made of?

THOMASIN.

This fellow Litterly—our cousin—who sneaks into our park after a pretty face! You could do it, if you liked!

TWEENWAYES.

Do what?

THOMASIN.

You know a lot of bad language, naturally?

TWEENWAYES.

My grandfather was called Round-oath Reginald. His swearing made history.

THOMASIN.

I know *some* too, only the mater bars that. Well, when you come across Litterly again, you use *yours*, will you?

TWEENWAYES.

[*Apprehensively.*] To Litterly?

THOMASIN.

Certainly, tell him what we all think of his conduct!

TWEENWAYES.

I—I should have little hesitation—er—in——

THOMASIN.

Good man! [*Running across to the right.*] Hullo!

TWEENWAYES.

Eh? Eh?

THOMASIN.

Here he is — with Noel. [TWEENWAYES *hastily makes for the thicket.*] No, no, not that way—over here.

NOELINE *and* LITTERLY *enter below the hedge, talking.* LITTERLY *carries* NOELINE'S *gun which he ultimately places against the hollow tree.*

NOELINE.

[*Embarrassed at encountering* THOMASIN *and* TWEEN-

WAYES.] Er—Tommy—this is Lord Litterly. [*To* LITTERLY.] My brother—sister—Thomasin.
[LITTERLY *bows to* THOMASIN, *who inclines her head stiffly and then turns her shoulder upon him.*

THOMASIN.

[*To* NOEL.] My friend, Lord Tweenwayes. [*To* TWEENWAYES] My brother Noel.
[TWEENWAYES *bows;* NOELINE *returns his salute haughtily.*

NOELINE.

[*Taking* THOMASIN *aside.*] Why do you treat Lord Litterly, a cousin, so very coolly?

THOMASIN.

[*To* NOELINE.] How dare he come here!

NOELINE.

He chances to be the young man who was useful to me in London.

THOMASIN.

Gracious! The creature who dangled you like a baby!

NOELINE.

Be silent! He has the good taste to gloss over that. Where's Willy?

THOMASIN.

With André de Grival.

NOELINE.

You're behaving like blackguards, both of you. Fetch your brother at once.

THOMASIN.

[*Going through the gate.*] Certainly. Our friends have tea with us, you may like to hear.

NOELINE.

Oh, the idea of such a thing!

THOMASIN.

Are you going to ask Litterly?

NOELINE.

It would be a marked impoliteness not to do so.

THOMASIN.

I thought as much!

NOELINE.

I'll box your ears to-night!

THOMASIN.

Noel, if you domineer, when I get indoors I—I—I'll be perfectly uncontrollable.

NOELINE.

[*Turning away.*] Impudent fellow!
 [THOMASIN *goes off.* TWEENWAYES *advances towards* LITTERLY *who is sitting on the root of the tree.*

TWEENWAYES.

[*Finding he is alone with* LITTERLY.] Er—Litterly—have you considered whether it is quite the act of a gentleman to—to—rove about a place where, for family reasons, it is obviously—ah—undesirable—eh?

LITTERLY.

My dear chap, I haven't thought at all about it. [*Glaring at* TWEENWAYES.] Have *you?*

TWEENWAYES.

[*Mildly.*] No, *I* haven't. [*He turns and goes through the gate irresolutely, looking to the right.*] Herefords!
 [*He quickly turns to the left, and disappears.*

NOEL *and* LITTERLY *approach each other rather constrainedly.*

LITTERLY.

[*Looking at his watch.*] I say, Lady Noeline, is the four forty-five a decent train?

NOELINE.

[*Indifferently.*] You return by it?

LITTERLY.

Bound to; I dine out to-night.

NOELINE.

Then I won't press you to wait for tea.

LITTERLY.

Tea!

NOELINE.
Tea comes down from the Hall directly.

LITTERLY.
Hang the train! It's only a man's dinner.

NOELINE.
[*Coldly.*] You mustn't disappoint your friends. Good-bye. [*He grips her hand tightly, and she cries out.*] Oh!

LITTERLY.
What?

NOELINE.
[*Holding her wrist.*] I have a sprained wrist.

LITTERLY.
[*Taking her hand again.*] I say, I am sorry! I'm afraid I—[*Looking at a mark upon her wrist.*] Hullo! What's that?

NOELINE.
Nothing.

LITTERLY.
N.

NOELINE.
My initial.

LITTERLY.
What's it doing there?

NOELINE.
I am sure you'll lose your train.

LITTERLY
Who put it there?
NOELINE.

[*Impatiently.*] Oh, when we were quite small boys—Willy and Tommy and I—we used to tattoo each other on wet days. The nearest way to the station——

LITTERLY.

[*Looking at her wrist.*] By Jove! how did you manage it?

NOELINE.

Oh dear, oh dear! If you must know, there's a scrubby little plant with a scarlet sap, growing here at Overcote, that does it. [*Walking about, looking upon the ground.*] It's early for it, but I daresay I can find you a sprout. [*Plucking a root.*] Yes, this is it, I believe. [*Breaking the stalk and showing it to him.*] There! You simply make punctures and paint them with the sap. [*He takes a sprig and examines it.*] The nearest way to Scrumleigh station——

LITTERLY.

[*Looking at his wrist, then at her.*] Would you mind carving something on me?

NOELINE.

I! [*Drawing herself up.*] Really!

LITTERLY.

I say, do! I say——

NOELINE.

[*Stamping her foot.*] What a maddening trick you

have of saying "I say"! Forgive me for remarking it.

LITTERLY.

I know; it's a rotten habit. I say—— [*Correcting himself.*] I beg your pardon—I mean, if you'd write me just one little letter——

NOELINE.

Lord Litterly!

LITTERLY.

On my wrist—it would remind me to drop saying "I say."

NOELINE.

[*Haughtily.*] I fear the habit must remain unchecked.

[*She walks away, and, with her back to him, picks some more of the plant.*

LITTERLY.

[*To himself, pulling the sprig to pieces.*] She hates me like poison—she hates me not—she——! I've half a mind to pay her out for snubbing me like this. I could do it too, if I chose to tell her of that trifling little circumstance I kept back. Ha, ha, ha! Why shouldn't I? Ha, ha! She hates me like rats—she hates me not. [*To* NOELINE.] Lady Noeline——

NOELINE.

[*Not turning.*] Yes?

LITTERLY.

I say, there's something on my conscience I should like to get rid of before I go.

NOELINE.
On your conscience?

LITTERLY.
Well, when I told you the tale of my picking-up that nice young fellow the night before last, I left out one little occurrence——

NOELINE.
You—left out—one little—occurrence!

LITTERLY.
It happened while his brain was wandering, just as we—but, very likely, you wouldn't think it belongs to the story.

NOELINE.
Perhaps you will give me the opportunity of judging.

LITTERLY.
With pleasure—on one condition.

NOELINE.
What's that?

LITTERLY.
[*Tapping his wrist.*] That you'll write me that letter.

NOELINE.
Certainly not.

LITTERLY.
As a memorial of an awfully jolly adventure.

NOELINE.
And that would be the price of the omitted episode?

LITTERLY.
[*Turning up his shirt cuff.*] The reserve price.

NOELINE.
I wouldn't pay it to buy the whole county!

LITTERLY.
[*Turning down his shirt cuff.*] Episode bought in.

NOELINE.
[*Fiercely.*] Oh! [*Irresolutely.*] You have really something to tell?

LITTERLY.
Honour bright.

NOELINE.
I—I think your behaviour is infamous. [*Drawing a long silver pin from her hair and approaching him.*] You have no objection to this?

LITTERLY.
[*Turning up his cuff again.*] Delighted.
[*She sits on the stump and he stands on her left extending his wrist.*

NOELINE.
What letter?

LITTERLY.
N will do.

NOELINE.
I prefer any other letter, please.

LITTERLY.
Oh, N stands for lots of things. N's for nothing.

NOELINE.

[*Angrily.*] Oh! [*She makes the punctures.*]

LITTERLY.

[*Sitting beside her.*] You can't reach.

NOELINE.

[*As she makes the punctures.*] This—will be—a vile —N—I promise you.

LITTERLY.

[*Wincing.*] You must have been plucky kids to stand much of this.

NOELINE.

[*Becoming interested in her work.*] We were—plucky kids—as you express it—Tommy especially.

LITTERLY.

Tommy?

NOELINE.

I remember—it was on Tommy—I used to make— the most—elaborate designs.

LITTERLY.

Poor Tommy! and have those frescoes faded?

NOELINE.

I think you are the most inquisitive person I have ever met.

LITTERLY.

Sorry.

NOELINE.

No, I wish they would die out; they occasion such serious inconvenience now.

LITTERLY.

Do they—how?

NOELINE.

Oh, really, if you will know everything, when Thomasin visits as a girl it is impossible for her to appear to advantage at dances or any low-necked function. [*Sticking the hairpin in her coat.*] There! [*Rubbing the broken stalk of the plant upon his wrist.*] I wish you joy of this N! [*They rise.*

NOELINE.

[*Listening.*] I think the others are coming. What is it you left out of your story? Be quick, please!

LITTERLY.

[*Turning down his cuff.*] I shouldn't have mentioned it only I think a chap who's fond of his mother must have a lot of good in him, and so it's no more than just to that Johnnie——

NOELINE.

Fond of his mother! Explain yourself!

LITTERLY.

Well, after I'd carried him up those seven-and-twenty stairs—

NOELINE.

[*Clenching her hands.*] Oh! Yes?

LITTERLY.

After I'd carried him up those stairs I stopped for wind on the landing. And it was then that nice young fellow sighed and groaned and put his arm round my neck——

NOELINE.

He didn't!

LITTERLY.

And called me " mother " in a whisper. He didn't know what he was up to, of course, but it showed his good instincts.

NOELINE.

Any—anything more?

LITTERLY.

One thing more. I couldn't stop his doing it, you know; my own arms were engaged.

NOELINE.

Stop his—doing what?

LITTERLY.

As he said " Good-night, mother," in a dreamy way, he kissed me. That's the incident. When's tea?

NOELINE.

Oh! Oh!
  [*She turns upon him fiercely, deals him a sounding blow upon his ear, and walks away.*

LITTERLY.

[*Looking after her.*] Does the invitation to tea still hold good?

WILHELMINA, DE GRIVAL, *and* THOMASIN *come through the gate.*

WILHELMINA.

[*With* DE GRIVAL *timidly.*] Noel, may I introduce Monsieur de Grival?

DE GRIVAL.

[*Advancing to* NOEL *gallantly.*] Lady Noeline, I am charmed to be here not asked.

THOMASIN.

[*Opening the gate.*] The tea! [*Calling.*] Look sharp, Youatt! Don't go to sleep, Fitton!

LITTERLY *is presented to* WILHELMINA. YOUATT *and* FITTON *enter through the gate, carrying a large square basket and some camp-stools. They open the basket and arrange the tea-things on the tree-stump,* THOMASIN *assisting, while* LITTERLY *busies himself in placing the camp-stools. After the tea is laid* YOUATT *removes the basket and takes up a position by the gate.* FITTON *goes off.*

THOMASIN.

[*To* YOUATT, *while tea is being laid.*] What's the matter with you, Youatt?

YOUATT.

[*Wagging his head.*] Oh, m'lord, what are we all a' comin' to!

THOMASIN.

We're all a' comin' to tea directly.

YOUATT.

Oh, the disgrace to the Park!

THOMASIN.

Youatt, if you ever breathe a word to a soul——!

YOUATT.

Don't think it o' me, m'lord.

LITTERLY.

[*To* THOMASIN, *who is carrying camp-stools.*] I say, let me help.

THOMASIN.

[*Glaring at him.*] Thanks, awfully.

LITTERLY.

[*To himself.*] The little 'un's no friend of mine.

THOMASIN.

[*To herself.*] Impudent interloper!

LITTERLY.

[*To himself.*] Rude little mass of tattoo!

THOMASIN.

[*Aloud.*] Tea! tea! Come along, Noel! Sit down, Willy! There you are, Monsieur de Grival!
  [*The girls sit upon the camp-stools, the men upon the ground—*NOEL *pouring out tea, with* LITTERLY *on her left;* THOMASIN *is in the centre, with* WILHELMINA *and* DE GRIVAL *on her right.*

G

YOUATT.

[*To himself.*] Ah, a sad stain on the park!

LITTERLY.

[*To* NOELINE, *wrapping his handkerchief round his wrist.*] You observe I am stopping to tea?

NOELINE.

[*To* LITTERLY, *disdainfully.*] I can hardly avoid doing so. Ah, please don't draw attention to your wrist in that way!

LITTERLY.

[*Putting his handkerchief away.*] I say, did my cousin Thomasin tingle like this when she was frescoed? [*Wincing.*] Oh!

THOMASIN.

[*Looking about.*] Where's Tweenwayes?

LITTERLY.

Yes, where's Tweeny?

DE GRIVAL.

Where is my friend Tweenwayes?

THOMASIN.

[*Calling.*] Lord Tweenwayes! Lord Tweenwayes!

LITTERLY.

[*Calling loudly.*] Halloa! Tweeny!

DE GRIVAL.

Tweenwayes!

TWEENWAYES.

[*In the distance.*] Coming!
          [*He crawls out of the thicket.*

THOMASIN.

Tea!

TWEENWAYES.

[*Sitting.*] Thank you.
          [YOUATT *comes and hands the tea.*

THOMASIN.

[*Quietly to* TWEENWAYES.] Tweeny, have you spoken your mind to Litterly yet?

TWEENWAYES.

I thought of waiting till I get him in town. We always deliberate before expressing our views.

THOMASIN.

Well, then, you must arrange with me exactly what you're going to say. Look here, will you and André de Grival come up to the Hall to-night, when it's dark, and have a quiet chat about it with Willy and me?

TWEENWAYES.

Come up to the Hall!

THOMASIN.

Not to the door, of course. You'll have to lower yourselves through a skylight. I'll write you out instructions.
      [TWEENWAYES *produces a letter, tears off the half-sheet, and gives it to* THOMASIN, *who*

writes on it with pencil. There is the sound of the loosening of a string of WILHELMINA'S *guitar in the hollow of the tree.*

DE GRIVAL.

[*Starting up.*] Ah! What!

WILHELMINA.

A string of my guitar!

DE GRIVAL.

[*Taking the guitar-case from the tree.*] Oh, you play, you sing!

WILHELMINA.

No, no!

DE GRIVAL.

[*Taking the guitar from the case.*] Lady Noeline, my dear Barrington, Tweenwayes—persuade! [*Handing the guitar to* WILHELMINA.] Don'cher know!

LITTERLY.

Lady Wilhelmina!

NOELINE.

Do, Willy.

DE GRIVAL.

[*Entreatingly.*] Ah, if you like!

[WILHELMINA *strikes a chord.*

TWEENWAYES.

[*To himself, writhing.*] We loathe music.

[WILHELMINA *sings a simple song in two verses.*

LITTERLY.

[*At the end of the first verse.*] I say, charming!

DE GRIVAL.

[*In ecstasy.*] Ah, bravo, bravo! Pretty good!

THOMASIN.

[*Quietly to* YOUATT, *giving him the note she has written.*] Take this to Monsieur de Grival.
[YOUATT *gives the note to* DE GRIVAL, *who reads it.* WILHELMINA *sings the second verse of the song, and is applauded.*

THOMASIN.

[*Quietly to* TWEENWAYES.] I've given André de Grival written directions how to—how to call upon us.

TWEENWAYES.

[*Glaring at* DE GRIVAL.] Why to him?

THOMASIN.

Don't you like him?

TWEENWAYES.

We—we are accustomed to take the lead in such matters.

NOELINE.

[*To everybody.*] Any more tea? Lord Tweenwayes, Lord Litterly, Monsieur de Grival?
[*The men decline.* NOELINE *rises, and they all follow.* TWEENWAYES *quietly disappears.* NOELINE *and* LITTERLY *stand together.* FITTON *re-enters; he and* YOUATT *replace*

the tea-things in the basket, fold the camp-stools and finally deposit them on the basket, then YOUATT *goes off through the gate and* FITTON *goes away to the left.*

LITTERLY.

[*To* NOEL.] Lady Noeline, permit me to thank you for a most delightful day.

NOELINE.

Delightful! You are still nursing your arm, I see.

LITTERLY.

[*Cheerfully.*] My arm is exceedingly painful—I wouldn't lose a throb of it.

NOELINE.

I—I struck you, I'm afraid.

LITTERLY.

There's a singing in my ear—but it's your voice.

NOELINE.

Perhaps I—I ought to apologise for losing my temper. Please forget it.

LITTERLY.

No, don't deprive me even of the recollection of—your temper.

WILHELMINA.

[*To* DE GRIVAL, *who is replacing the guitar in the tree.*] Good-bye, Monsieur de Grival.

THOMASIN.

[*To* WILHELMINA.] No, no. He's coming up to the Hall by-and-bye with Tweeny, to have a smoke and a chat with you and me.

WILHELMINA.

[*Horrified.*] Tommy!

NOELINE.

Now boys! Where are the guns?
[*The guns are collected, and* WILHELMINA, THOMASIN, *and* NOEL *stand together, guns in hand.*]

NOELINE.

We've just time to walk through Silverthorn Coppice before dusk. [*Taking her place between* WILHELMINA *and* THOMASIN.] Gentleman, a final word. [*Looking round.*] Where is Lord Tweenwayes.

THOMASIN.

[*Calling.*] Tweenwayes!

LITTERLY.

Tweeny!

DE GRIVAL.

Tweenwayes, my friend!

ALL.

Tweenwayes!

[TWEENWAYES *enters from below the hedge. A red flush suffuses his nose and cheeks.*]

WILHELMINA.

Oh, dear!

THOMASIN.
Queer, Tweeny?
TWEENWAYES.
We ought never to take tea.

NOELINE.
Gentlemen, my brothers and I bid you good afternoon.
THOMASIN.
Good-afternoon.
WILHELMINA.
Good-afternoon.
NOELINE.
We have been extremely wrong in receiving you here.
THOMASIN.
[*Emphatically.*] Yes.
NOELINE.
You are almost equally to blame for permitting us to do so.
WILHELMINA.
Ah, yes.
THOMASIN.
No doubt about that!
NOELINE.
We ask you to forget that you have entered Overcote Park. In a few hours the grass will revive where you have trodden—let that be a hint to your memories.

Now be kind enough to leave the park at once. Good-bye.
> [*The men advance together and shake hands with the girls.*

LITTERLY.

Thanks for a splendid time.

TWEENWAYES.

Most interesting day.

DE GRIVAL.

Ah, I have liked myself here!
> [*The men return to their places, raising their hats as the girls go through the gate.*

NOELINE.

Where's Fitton?

THOMASIN.

Jo!

WILHELMINA.

He'll follow.

NOELINE.

Come, boys!
> [*They disappear. Sunset appears.* LITTERLY *sits thoughtfully;* TWEENWAYES *and* DE GRIVAL *stand together, eyeing him.*

DE GRIVAL.

[*To* TWEENWAYES.] What to do? How to give Barrington the slip?

TWEENWAYES.

[*To* DE GRIVAL.] We simply leave the park now with him and walk to the station.

DE GRIVAL.
Don'cher know?

TWEENWAYES.
It will be easy to invent an excuse for our not sharing his compartment. For instance, he will smoke.

DE GRIVAL.
Ah, necessity is the mother of objecting to a smoking-carriage!

TWEENWAYES.
Just as the train is starting we two get out and speed back to Overcote.

DE GRIVAL.
My friend! How quick the brain!

TWEENWAYES.
We are seldom at a loss. [*Advancing to* LITTERLY.] You catch the next train, I presume, Litterly?

LITTERLY.
[*Indifferently.*] Oh, I catch it or lose it. [*To himself.*] She's glorious!

TWEENWAYES.
[*Annoyed.*] De Grival and I catch it.

LITTERLY.
- Good luck, old chaps. [*To himself.*] She's splendid!

TWEENWAYES.
It would have been pleasant for us all to have finished the day together.

LITTERLY.

Don't bother about me; I may stroll about and go back later.

[DE GRIVAL *and* TWEENWAYES *retire and consult together.*

DE GRIVAL.

[*To* TWEENWAYES.] What to do?

TWEENWAYES.

[*Vaguely.*] We are seldom at a loss.

DE GRIVAL.

Your plan has broken up.

TWEENWAYES.

Dash it, manage it yourself!

DE GRIVAL.

[*Coming to* LITTERLY.] My dear Barrington, our word to the ladies. Honesty is the best way out of the park. [*Taking* TWEENWAYES' *arm.*] Tweenwayes and I now go.

LITTERLY.

[*Rising.*] Oh, which way?

DE GRIVAL.

The way we entered.

LITTERLY.

All right—run along.

DE GRIVAL.

[*To* LITTERLY.] Which way do you?

LITTERLY.

The way *I* entered. [*Waving his hand.*] See you soon.

DE GRIVAL.

[*Waving his hand.*] A pleasant picnic together! Good-bye!

LITTERLY.

[*Taking out a cigarette.*] Ta, ta!

TWEENWAYES.

[*Glaring at* LITTERLY.] He drops us! Insolent!
[TWEENWAYES *and* DE GRIVAL *go off, arm-in-arm, below the hedge.* LITTERLY *espies* THOMASIN'S *note which* DE GRIVAL *has dropped by the tree.*

LITTERLY.

[*Picking up the note.*] Hullo! [*Reading.*] " Dear M. de Grival. Am asking you and Tweenwayes to come up to the Hall when dark to see me and Billy and to talk about snubbing this horrid Litterly, who no one excepting Noel likes poking his nose about our park." Illiterate little beast! [*Resuming.*] " We can't entertain you tip-top, as it must be in our old shut-up schoolroom, but there will be a decent weed and, please Heaven, sloes in brandy. The following is the way in." [*Looking after* TWEENWAYES *and* DE GRIVAL.] " Confound 'em!" [*Resuming.*] " Skirt the lawn and make for East Wing. Clamber on to red-tiled lean-to outhouse. From there on to roof of dwarf tower. Find the skylight. Lift up skylight and drop through. Wait in the dark till we turn up. Tweeny has accepted. Keep your eye on him when on the roof as he is a bit gone over at the knees. Yours up to date T. Belturbet." Designing little mass of tattoo! I say, by Jove, I'll play the dooce with these fellows!

[DE GRIVAL *runs up, scared, hatless, and disordered.*

DE GRIVAL.

My dear Barrington!

LITTERLY.

[*Slipping the note into his pocket.*] Hullo!

DE GRIVAL.

We have encountered—not a pirate—no, no, a poacher. We are hurt.

LITTERLY.

Where's Tweenwayes?

TWEENWAYES *enters. His hat is crushed down over his eyes, his clothes are torn, and generally he presents evidence of having been engaged in a struggle.*

DE GRIVAL.

[*Embracing* TWEENWAYES.] My friend!

LITTERLY.

[*Pulling* DE GRIVAL *away.*] What have they been doing to you, Tweeny?

TWEENWAYES.

Just as we got to the brook—great hulking brute—

putting down nets—never heard such language in my life—wanted to know why an honest man wasn't allowed to earn a living. I said we never answered questions of that sort——

DE GRIVAL.

My head!

TWEENWAYES.

Yes, yes, the wretch knocked De Grival's head against mine, twice.

DE GRIVAL.

Three times.

TWEENWAYES.

Possibly. I left off counting. Luckily somebody came up and enabled us to get away. A poaching beast!

LITTERLY.

Come on, you chaps!

TWEENWAYES.

[*Detaining* LITTERLY.] No, no, don't interfere—he's choking the keeper. [LITTERLY *runs off.*] Oh, it's a filthy park!

DE GRIVAL.

[*Leaning against a tree.*] My head is a very bad one.

TWEENWAYES.

[*Feeling his leg.*] We can't stand being knocked about. Heavens, this limb is injured!

DE GRIVAL.

Did you see me kick him.

TWEENWAYES.

Kick him!

DE GRIVAL.

The poacher—I thought I had broken him.

TWEENWAYES.

Fool! that was my leg!

[ORTS, *a most forbidding-looking rustic, emerges from the thicket.*

DE GRIVAL.

[*Turning.*] Ah!

ORTS.

Theer 'ee be agen! Git 'ee out of my way! [*Flinging* DE GRIVAL *to the ground and dealing* TWEENWAYES *a blow which knocks him down.*] I be a poor agricultural labourer. Gi' me all the goold you've got on 'ee!

TWEENWAYES.

[*Emptying his pockets.*] Oh, this is an atrocious park! [*Giving his money to* ORTS.] Go away!

ORTS.

Farmin' be bad in these parts, I tell 'ee. This beaint all!

TWEENWAYES.

[*Faintly.*] We never carry much loose money.

ORTS.

Then I'll blacken thy other eye for 'ee!

TWEENWAYES.

My friend changed a note this morning! Try my friend!
[ORTS *turns to* DE GRIVAL, *who commences to search for his money.*

ORTS.

[*To* DE GRIVAL.] I tell 'ee I be thoroughly deservin'! Thy goold!

LITTERLY *enters from below the hedge, followed by* FITTON. *He seizes* ORTS *and pinions him from behind.*

LITTERLY.

[*To* FITTON.] Your belt, Fitton! Do you know the scoundrel?
[FITTON *takes a strap from his waist; and he and* LITTERLY *secure* ORTS'S *arms.*

FITTON.

John Orts, m'lord; a poacher since he were a babby!

ORTS.

I be the sole support o' my mother, I be. Not a single Sunday marnin' sarvice 'ave I missed at Scrumleigh church this ten year.

LITTERLY.

Now then, Fitton, what shall we do?

FITTON.

[*To* LITTERLY.] If we make p'lice business o' this

m'lord, it'll come out theer's been some rakes about th' park arter our young gentlemen. Folks will be talking.

LITTERLY.

[*To* FITTON.] That's true. Better run the scoundrel off the place and have done with him.

TWEENWAYES.

[*Faintly.*] Another moment and I should have had his name and address.

LITTERLY.

[*To* FITTON.] Put my friends on their legs. [*To* ORTS.] Get on!

ORTS.

[*Going.*] I were i' th' church choir five year, singin' loike a cherrybim.

[*He disappears,* LITTERLY *following him.*

FITTON.

[*Raising* TWEENWAYS.] Hey, thy left eye be a rum 'un.

[TWEENWAYES *sits on the stump of a tree; his eye is slightly discoloured.* FITTON *picks up* DE GRIVAL.

TWEENWAYES.

[*Almost in tears.*] Heavens, what a park!

DE GRIVAL.

[*To* FITTON.] A doctor very near? Tell me.

FITTON.

If it be only bruises, sir, Bowser, High Street, Scrumleigh, Chemist and Druggist.

H

DE GRIVAL.

[*To* TWEENWAYES.] My friend, let us go and be drugged. [*Looking at* TWEENWAYES, *who rises.*] Ah, a great change in you.

TWEENWAYES.

We scar quickly.

DE GRIVAL.

[*Taking his arm.*] It is a wise father who knows his own friend when he has such a bad eye.

[TWEENWAYES *and* DE GRIVAL *disappear. After a brief pause,* DE GRIVAL *returns.*]

DE GRIVAL.

[*Calling to* TWEENWAYES.] In a moment I come after you. [*To* FITTON, *hurriedly.*] Mister what-your-name, I did not rescue you from that pirate—that poacher?

FITTON.

[*Touching his cap.*] No, sir, that I swear ye didn't.

DE GRIVAL.

No—but it would not hurt you to swear I did.

FITTON.

Well, sir——

DE GRIVAL.

Listen to me. [*Taking a handful of money from his pocket.* TWEENWAYES *re-entering unperceived, steals down suspiciously, and stands behind* DE GRIVAL *and* FITTON, *listening.*] You go to Lady Wilhelmina directly, at once. [*Giving him money.*] One sovereign. You tell her of this affair. [*Giving him money.*] Two pound. You say I found that poacher strangling your throat. [*Giving him money.*] Another. You tell Lady Wilhelmina I kick him, I rescue you, I kick you —no, no, I kick him again. I save your life, ah, bravely! [*Giving him more money.*] Don'cher know!

TWEENWAYES.

[*Coming between* FITTON *and* DE GRIVAL.] Monsieur de Grival!

DE GRIVAL.

Ah!

TWEENWAYES.

Permit me to say that, if any representation of this kind is made—*I*—I must be——

DE GRIVAL.

In *it?* [TWEENWAYES *bows with dignity.*] I have no objection.

TWEENWAYES.

[*To* FITTON.] You will see Lady Thomasin as well as Lady Wilhelmina. [*Searching his pockets.*] Monsieur de Grival and *I* found the poacher choking you This gentleman and *I*, at great personal risk, preserved your—heavens, that villain has my money!

DE GRIVAL.

Ah! [*Producing money and offering it to* TWEEN-WAYES.] I loan you.

TWEENWAYES.

[*To himself, hesitating.*] Can I? [*Taking the money and giving it to* FITTON.] You understand?

FITTON.

[*Touching his cap.*] Yes, m'lord.
[TWEENWAYES *moves away.*

DE GRIVAL.

[*To* FITTON, *pointing to* TWEENWAYES.] We now save your life, both of us, ah, bravely! Don'cher know?

FITTON.

I know, sir.

DE GRIVAL.

[*Going to* TWEENWAYES.] We reconcile each other? [TWEENWAYES *reluctantly extends two fingers.* DE GRIVAL *cheerfully takes his arm again.*] My friend!
[*They go off. It is now dusk.*

FITTON.

[*Counting his money.*] Dang it, it won't do me no hurt tellin' a few lies about 'un. Two—three—four.

LITTERLY *re-enters.*

LITTERLY.

Where are my friends, Fitton?

FITTON.

[*Pocketing the money.*] They be just gone.

LITTERLY.

[*To himself, chuckling.*] By Jove, I mean to play Old Harry with 'em! Ha, ha, ha! [*Sitting and holding his arm.*] Oh, I say!

FITTON.

Twisted thy arm, m'lord?

LITTERLY.

[*Taking out his pocket-handkerchief.*] Fitton, wrap this handkerchief round my wrist, as tightly as you can. [*To himself.*] Ho, ho, these fellows!

FITTON.

[*Looking at* LITTERLY'S *arm.*] Eh, the scoundrel's hurt'ee!

LITTERLY.

No, no, Lady Noeline was kind enough to do that with a hair-pin and a red root that grows about the park. Lady Noeline and I are cousins, you know, Fitton. Go on.

FITTON.

[*Blankly.*] A red root that grows hereabouts.

LITTERLY.

Yes. [*Putting his foot on a piece of the root which lies on the ground.*] Here's a bit of it.

FITTON.

[*Picking up the root.*] That?

NOELINE.

[*In the distance calling.*] Joe! Halloa! Fitton!

FITTON.

[*Going to the gate.*] The young gentlemen be on their way back to the Hall.

LITTERLY *hastily conceals himself behind a tree.* NOEL *enters.*

NOELINE.

[*Stopping at the gate.*] Fitton, why do you leave us like this ?

FITTON.

[*To* NOEL, *over the gate.*] 'Scuse me, m'lord—[*showing the sprig he has in his hand*]—be that the weed you've been ruddling young Lord Latterby's arm wi' ?

NOELINE.

Who told you anything about that ? Take my gun ; I'm going home.

FITTON.

M'lord, this be the wrong stuff, I tell'ee.

NOELINE.

Eh ?

FITTON.

The Red Root hasn't grown here at Overcote many a year. This 'ere be crimson snake-wort ; it be a rank bad poison, they do tell me.

NOELINE.

[*Coming through the gate.*] Fitton !

FITTON.

[*Looking towards the tree.*] Sssh !

NOELINE.

Fitton, you don't mean—to say—I've really hurt my cousin's arm !

FITTON.

Lord Latterby, m'lord.
  [NOEL *sees* LITTERLY. FITTON *goes quietly away*. LITTERLY *advances to* NOEL.

NOELINE.

[*Agitatedly.*] Oh, Lord Litterly——!

LITTERLY.

I say, here's a game!

NOELINE.

A game! Don't stand there looking at me! Get out of the park! Why did you ever come here! Go—go to Doctor Flack at Great Overcote! Don't you hear me! [*Shaking him.*] Run—run to Doctor Flack!

LITTERLY.

[*Calmly.*] Why, I've never been to a doctor in my life.

NOELINE.

[*Faintly.*] You must now. [*Clinging to him.*] Oh! oh!

LITTERLY.

[*Supporting her, soothingly.*] Don't! don't! Ah, I know how to hold you!

NOELINE.

[*Getting away.*] How dare you! I—I hate you!

LITTERLY.

Do you! Then I swear to go to no doctor!

NOELINE.

Pshaw! What do I care! It serves you right. [*Going up to the gate and opening it; while he sits whistling. Then hesitating and returning to him.*] Lord Litterly——!

LITTERLY.

Hullo!

NOELINE.

Won't anything make you go to the doctor?

LITTERLY.

Yes, tell me you don't hate me.

NOELINE.

[*After a pause.*] I don't hate you.
[*He rises and clasps her in his arms.* THOMASIN *and* WILHELMINA *enter, followed by* FITTON.

THOMASIN.

[*At the gate.*] Noel! [NOELINE *and* LITTERLY *separate. Meeting* LITTERLY *and speaking fiercely.*] What do you mean by this?

LITTERLY.

[*Triumphantly.*] Ha, ha! Cousin Tommy!
[*He throws his arms round* THOMASIN *and kisses her. She screams in a very feminine way. He runs off.*

THOMASIN.

[*Rubbing her face vigorously with her handkerchief*

and speaking to NOELINE.] You—you——! Do you call yourself a man !

NOELINE.

No ! I'm a girl ! I don't want to be anything else ! [*She runs off, through the open gate.* WILHELMINA, THOMASIN *and* FITTON *remain looking after her.*

END OF THE SECOND ACT.

THE THIRD ACT

The scene is a gymnasium at Overcote Hall—a large apartment artistically decorated and fitted with gymnastic apparatus. Halfway up the room is an arch, which, supported on two pilasters, divides the ceiling from the sky-lights. A door on the left opens on to a passage, while on the right is the door of a spacious cupboard. A vaulting horse, a suspended rope, parallel bars and a horizontal bar are prominent features of the apartment, while there are also a settee, table, and upright pianoforte. The place is in darkness, but a faint blue is seen through the sky-lights and the large window at the end of the room. After a short silence, there are the sounds of men's voices in whispers and the breaking of glass; then a man's hat drops from above, and DE GRIVAL *is seen descending, with difficulty, with the aid of the rope.*

DE GRIVAL.

[*In a whisper to* TWEENWAYES, *who is above.*] Tweenwayes, my friend, be careful; it is not easy.

TWEENWAYES.

[*Out of sight.*] Oh! look out! I'm descending! [*Coming down.*] Hold the thing! hold it!

DE GRIVAL.

Hold where?

TWEENWAYES.

[*Nearly down.*] The rope! [*He falls.*] Ah! [*Under his breath.*] Fool! fool!

DE GRIVAL.

You are hurt!

TWEENWAYES.

[*Crawling along.*] Heavens, yes!

[DE GRIVAL *picks him up. Their appearance is very dilapidated.* DE GRIVAL'S *clothes are soiled, his hair has become lank, and there is a star-shaped patch of white plaster on his brow.* TWEENWAYES *wears a small black shade over his injured eye.*

DE GRIVAL.

One thing we may congratulate ourselves—we arrive.

TWEENWAYES.

Arrive! How can I be certain that we have strictly carried out Lady Thomasin's instructions? The mere idea of your losing that note fills me with——[*Walking against the vaulting horse.*] Oh!

DE GRIVAL.

My friend, what is done cannot be made different. [*Coming into contact with the support of the horizontal bar.*] Ah! damitall!

TWEENWAYES.

[*Examining the vaulting horse and the horizontal bar*

with the aid of his magnifying glass.] De Grival, I have a shocking misgiving.

DE GRIVAL.

Misgiving?

TWEENWAYES.

Heavens, I believe we're in the Gymnasium!

DE GRIVAL.

Gymnasium!

TWEENWAYES.

Our instincts are rarely at fault. [*Coming against the parallel bars.*] Oh!

DE GRIVAL.

You are hurt?

TWEENWAYES.

Yes.

DE GRIVAL.

But I remember Lady Thomasin's letter, every word of it. [*Holding his head.*] "Clamber on to our old schoolroom . . . find a skylight in a roof . . . lift up the tiles of a outhouse . . . climb on to a tower . . . drop off and wait there till we turn up . . . yours, gone over at the knees, T. Belturbet."

[TWEENWAYES *falls over the Indian clubs; there is a great rattle.*

DE GRIVAL.

You are hurt again?

TWEENWAYES.

Yes. But wasn't there something about the West Wing? You said so.

DE GRIVAL.
Certainly, the West Wing. Or the—ah, I think!

TWEENWAYES.
You think!

DE GRIVAL.
My friend, pardon me—I fear I have changed a wing!

TWEENWAYES.
[*To himself.*] Fool! fool! [*Starting back as his hand drops on to the keys of the piano.*] Oh!

DE GRIVAL.
You are hurt!

TWEENWAYES.
No, I am not!

DE GRIVAL.
[*Joining him.*] What to do?

TWEENWAYES.
You may do what you please, Monsieur de Grival; so far as I am concerned, this visit to Overcote has come to a wretched close.
[*He goes to the rope, attempts to climb it, and fails.*]

DE GRIVAL.
[*Watching him.*] Ah, you cannot!

TWEENWAYES.
Heavens, it's beyond me! [*Sitting on the settee despondingly.*] What a horrible predicament! This

reminds me of many a page in our history. The dungeon, the prisoner. [*Rubbing his shins.*] Even the implements of torture!

DE GRIVAL.

[*Sitting beside him in great dejection.*] My spirits go.

TWEENWAYES.

We have no spirits.

DE GRIVAL.

[*Taking his hand.*] My friend!
  [*A pair of legs appear from above clinging to the rope.*]

TWEENWAYES *and* DE GRIVAL.

Oh!

DE GRIVAL.

[*In a whisper.*] What is it?

TWEENWAYES.

Surely, legs.

DE GRIVAL.

Ah, Wilhelmina!
  [*The legs descend and* LITTERLY *is revealed.*

DE GRIVAL.

[*Rising.*] Barrington!

TWEENWAYES.

[*Rising.*] Litterly!

LITTERLY.

Hullo! There you are!
[LITTERLY *comes between* DE GRIVAL *and* TWEENWAYES. *His arm is slung in a black silk handkerchief.*]

LITTERLY.

Now then, I should like to know what you've got to say for yourselves.

TWEENWAYES.

We never give explanations.

LITTERLY.

[*To* TWEENWAYES.] You catch the next train, don't you?

TWEENWAYES.

Really, this tone——!

LITTERLY.

It would be pleasant to finish the day together, wouldn't it? [*To* DE GRIVAL.] Our word to the ladies! Honesty is the best way out of the park! [*Taking* TWEENWAYES' *arm.*] Tweenwayes and I now go!

DE GRIVAL.

[*Penitently.*] My friend!

TWEENWAYES.

[*Releasing himself.*] You may not be aware, Litterly, that De Grival and I are here in the position of invited guests.

LITTERLY.

Oh, yes, I'm aware of it. [*Handing* THOMASIN'S *note to* DE GRIVAL.] I picked up the invitation.

DE GRIVAL *and* TWEENWAYES.

Ah!

LITTERLY.

And you may not be aware, my dear Tweeny, that that invitation directs you to the East Wing, and you are now in the West Wing.

TWEENWAYES.

Monsieur de Grival!

DE GRIVAL.

Ah, I commit an error! Pardon me!

TWEENWAYES.

Never! We never forgive an injury of this kind. [*To* LITTERLY.] How am I to get out?

LITTERLY.

The rope——

DE GRIVAL.

Bah! he cannot climb it!

TWEENWAYES.

Nor you, sir! [*Under his breath.*] Insolent!

DE GRIVAL.

You say so! I try!
[*He goes to the rope and attempts to climb it.*

LITTERLY.

[*Walking about.*] I've followed you fellows over about five miles of roof. Where the dooce have you got to? Why, I say, confound you, we're in the gym.!

TWEENWAYES.

I knew it! I felt it!

LITTERLY.

By Jove, this is too bad of us—we really ought to draw the line somewhere. [*Pointing to the door.*] Isn't that the door?

TWEENWAYES.

[*Opening the door cautiously.*] A passage. And lights at the end of it. [*Closing the door.*

LITTERLY.

[*Opening the opposite door.*] A cupboard.

DE GRIVAL.

[*Half-way up the rope.*] Ah, I succeed! I triumph! I do it! Don'cher know!

LITTERLY.

Bravo, André! We shall have to leave Tweeny behind us!

TWEENWAYES.

[*Under his breath.*] Insolent!
   [*The electric lights are switched on, and the scene becomes suddenly bright.* DE GRIVAL *descends precipitately.*

DE GRIVAL.

Ah!

TWEENWAYES.

Heavens!

LITTERLY.

I say!

TWEENWAYES.

Voices! voices!

LITTERLY.

[*At the cupboard door.*] Look out, you fellows!
  [DE GRIVAL *runs into the cupboard, and*
  LITTERLY *pushes in* TWEENWAYES, *who is
  hesitating, then goes in himself. After a
  brief pause, "Sergeant"* SHUTER *enters.
  She wears a costume of coarse, dark material,
  a blouse, a skirt finishing just below the
  knees, and gymnasium shoes.*

SHUTER.

[*At the door.*] Now then, m'lord! Where are the rest? A quarter-of-an-hour late as it is!

THOMASIN, WILHELMINA, *and* NOELINE *enter.
They are enveloped in long cloaks.*

What's the matter with you this evening? You all seem as stupid as owls, every one of you!

THOMASIN.

Don't you be cheeky, Sergeant, or I'll tell the mater.

SHUTER.

I'll tell her ladyship.

THOMASIN.
We're not inclined for the gym. to-night. There!

WILHELMINA.
We—we've had rather a tiring day, Sergeant.

SHUTER.
[*To* NOELINE, *who is leaning dejectedly against the vaulting-horse.*] Well, Lord Noel, if ever I did see anybody looking exactly like putty——!

NOELINE.
I don't care what I look like!

SHUTER.
[*Clapping her hands.*] Come along, now! Key, please! [NOELINE *locks the door and takes out the key. Bringing down the Indian clubs.*] I always have said that when your lordships come back from these wretched holiday-trips your muscles are like apple jelly.

NOELINE.
[*Throwing her the key*]. Catch and be quiet!
[SHUTER *catches the key and slips it into her pocket.*]

SHUTER.
[*Bringing down the bar bells.*] If I were m'lady I'd stop visitings altogether. [NOELINE *sits on the settee in an attitude of despondency.*] There's the result of it! I suppose you've been dancing half the night through in those petticoats of yours! Ah, I wonder you like

to wear such things! [*Bringing down the dumb bells.*]
Now then, Lord Tommy—Lord Willy!
 [WILHELMINA *and* THOMASIN *hurry forward
 sulkily.*

WILHELMINA *and* THOMASIN.

[*To themselves.*] Oh!

SHUTER.

[*Turning up her sleeves.*] Ten minutes' simple exercise to thaw the ice. Ready? [*Loudly*] Ready?

NOELINE.

[*Rising.*] Yes.

WILHELMINA.

Yes.

THOMASIN.

[*Loudly.*] Yes.

SHUTER.

Come, my lords! A good appetite for dinner!
 [SHUTER *sits at the piano and thumps out a
 strongly marked tune. The girls take off
 their cloaks and throw them down angrily;
 they are in elegantly-made gymnasium
 dresses of different colours.*

NOELINE.

[*Pushing* THOMASIN.] There's no room for me here.

THOMASIN.

[*Obstinately.*] This is my place.

NOELINE.

You're a most ungentlemanly fellow.

THOMASIN.
Because I caught you kissing Litterly!

NOELINE.
What——!

WILHELMINA.
[*Coming between them with the dumb bells in her hands.*] Oh, please don't quarrel again! Don't!

NOELINE.
Never interfere, Willy!

THOMASIN.
Out of the way, baby!
[WILHELMINA *is pushed over to the settee, where she sits crying and rubbing the dumb bells into her eyes.*

NOELINE.
[*To* THOMASIN.] At any rate, if I were to so far forget myself, 1 shouldn't be kissing a worm.

THOMASIN.
You allude to my friend Tweeny!

NOELINE.
[*Swinging her clubs.*] You seem—to have no doubt —as to whom—the denomination—applies.

THOMASIN.
[*Fiercely, as she picks up a bar-bell.*] Noel, do you remember my dropping a forty-pound bar-bell on to Shuter's toes, in the summer, by accident?

NOELINE.

Clumsy! Yes.

THOMASIN.

[*Lifting her bar-bell.*] Well—it wasn't an accident.

NOELINE.

Oh!

[SHUTER *abruptly discontinues playing and looks around.*

SHUTER.

Well, I never——! You—you——!

THOMASIN, WILHELMINA *and* NOELINE.

All right, Sergeant!

[*They commence their exercise.* SHUTER *resumes playing, with an occasional glance round. Keeping one eye on* SHUTER, THOMASIN *gets nearer to* WILHELMINA.

THOMASIN.

[*Speaking during her exercise to* WILHELMINA.] Billy, I wonder when we shall get to Tweeny and De Grival!

WILHELMINA.

[*To* THOMASIN.] Poor fellows, how lonely they must be in the dark!

THOMASIN.

I hope Tweeny hasn't broken a leg or anything.

WILHELMINA.

Oh, don't!

THOMASIN.
He looks a bit brittle.
[*Their exercise becomes languid.*

WILHELMINA.
It was awfully plucky of André, protecting Fitton from that poacher, wasn't it?

THOMASIN.
And Tweeny!

WILHELMINA.
I mean both.

THOMASIN.
What did Fitton tell you about it?
[*They cease their exercise altogether and, forgetting* SHUTER, *sit on the settee side-by-side.*

WILHELMINA.
Why, Fitton said that André lifted the poacher high in the air, like a baby.

THOMASIN.
That's right—and then threw him to Tweeny who caught him ten yards off.

WILHELMINA.
What did Tweenwayes do then?

THOMASIN.
Shook him blue and chucked him back to André.

WILHELMINA.

I shouldn't have thought Tweenwayes quite equal to all that.

THOMASIN.

Nor I—André. You never know men.

WILHELMINA.

[*Sadly.*] I suppose you oughtn't to. [NOELINE's *exercise has flagged by degrees; she now sits on the vaulting-horse with her back to the others.*] Just look at Noel!

THOMASIN.

I s'pose Noel calls that club exercise—*I* call it shirking.

WILHELMINA.

Tommy, it's an awful thing to realise, but, after what we saw, there can be no doubt that Noel l—l—likes Litterly, eh?

THOMASIN.

Doubt!

WILHELMINA.

Oh, things are getting pretty serious at Overcote, don't you think?

THOMASIN.

Billy, old chap, dashed if I know what the dooce is coming over us all!

WILHELMINA.

[*Sighing.*] Ah!
    [SHUTER *again suddenly ceases playing, turns, and rises.*

SHUTER.

I guessed it! [*In great commotion, the girls rush to their places and resume their exercise.*] I've caught you! Every bit of this shall go to m'lady. Now, my lords, no more nonsense, please! Back with those toys!

[*The girls replace the clubs, bar bells, and dumb bells at the further end of the room.*

THOMASIN.

[*To* WILHELMINA.] We've made the Sergeant wild now!

WILHELMINA.

And I've no chocolate in my pocket to get her round again!

SHUTER.

[*Gathering up the cloaks.*] Wiping the floor with these things too! Isn't there a proper place for them? Lord Noel, Lord Willy—on to the Bar, both of you! Lord Tommy, thirty vaults without stopping for wind!

[NOELINE *and* WILHELMINA *spring on to the horizontal-bar and* THOMASIN *comes to the vaulting-horse as* SHUTER, *carrying the cloaks, opens the cupboard door. The men appear ;* SHUTER, *dropping the cloaks, utters a yell of terror and runs over to the other side of the room. There is a general uproar, the girls scream,* TWEENWAYES *running across the room is seized by* SHUTER *and violently shaken. Escaping from her, he makes for the rope, where he meets* DE GRIVAL, *who has crawled under the vault-*

ing-horse; they attempt to climb the rope together, impeding each other's progress.

NOELINE.

It's Litterly!

WILHELMINA.

André de Grival!

THOMASIN.

Why, Tweeny!

LITTERLY.

Hush! hush! Come back, you fellows! Be quiet, everybody! I say, do let me speak!

SHUTER.

[*Going to* LITTERLY *and shaking him.*] Who are you all! What are you doing here?

[NOELINE *comes down quickly, places herself between* LITTERLY *and* SHUTER, *and seizes the latter by the collar.*

NOELINE.

You coward, Shuter! Don't you see Lord Litterly's arm is in a sling?

SHUTER.

[*Staring at* LITTERLY.] Lord Litterly! Oh, my lord!

LITTERLY.

[*Advancing to* SHUTER.] Hullo! Why—Letty!

SHUTER.

[*Hysterically.*] Oh, m'lord, what is the meaning of this?

LITTERLY.

I say, now don't upset yourself! I *am* glad to see you! [*Kissing her.*

NOELINE.

[*To* LITTERLY.] Do you know what you're doing? You're kissing our Sergeant!

LITTERLY.

I should think so! Letty Shuter is my old nurse's daughter; we were brought up together—Letty was married from Bambridge Castle! [*Kissing* SHUTER *again.*] I should think I *am* kissing your Sergeant! [*Quietly to* NOELINE.] Leave her to me—it's all right.
　　　　[THOMASIN, WILHELMINA, DE GRIVAL *and* TWEENWAYES *are talking together with much animation.* NOELINE *joins them.* SHUTER *sinks on to the settee holding her heart and panting;* LITTERLY *places himself beside her.*

LITTERLY.

I say, Letty dear, how jolly!

SHUTER.

Jolly! Oh dear, oh dear! I'll never get over this fright! [*Pushing him away and attempting to rise.*] You wretch!

LITTERLY.

[*Restraining her.*] What, when I haven't seen you for years!

SHUTER.

As if you came here to see me! Who are the others?

LITTERLY.

My friends, Lord Tweenwayes and Monsieur de Grival.

SHUTER.

My lords' sweethearts up in Scotland! I've heard of it!

[*She again attempts to rise; he pulls her back and puts his arm round her waist.*

LITTERLY.

Letty, I'll tell you something! Keep quiet! [*Whispering into her ear.*] I say——!

SHUTER.

What! Lord Noel! [*He nods, laughing.*] Oh, I won't help you, either of you!

[*She again tries to leave him; he rises and stands before her, pushing her back whenever she attempts to rise.*

LITTERLY.

Letty, be reasonable! What are you frightened about? If I give you my word that I will personally be answerable for the perfect behaviour of your young gentlemen, will that satisfy you?

SHUTER.

No!

LITTERLY.
Why, Lady Castlejordan's away, isn't she?

SHUTER.
She'll be home to-morrow.

LITTERLY.
But we don't intend to stay till to-morrow.

SHUTER.
I'll take care of that!

LITTERLY.
That's right, always do your duty. [*Looking at his watch.*] Now, at what time do your young gentlemen dine?

SHUTER.
A quarter-past eight.

LITTERLY.
Then at a quarter *to* eight we leave.

SHUTER.
On your honour, m'lord?

LITTERLY.
Letty, on my honour! [*She rises; he kisses her again and puts her back.*] I *am* pleased to see you. Gentlemen, at a quarter to eight punctually, we clear out. I have pledged my word to that effect to my dear old friend, Mrs. Shuter. So, I warn you, you must make the most of your time.

SHUTER.

[*Starting up.*] No, they mustn't!

WILHELMINA.

[*Running up to* SHUTER *and hugging her.*] Oh, Shuter, dear, you've never been so nice!

THOMASIN.

[*To* SHUTER.] Sergeant, you're a brick!

WILHELMINA.

Come and talk to Lord Tweenwayes and Monsieur de Grival; your mind will be *so* easy.

[THOMASIN *and* WILHELMINA *take* SHUTER *to* TWEENWAYES *and* DE GRIVAL.

NOELINE.

[*To* LITTERLY, *very coldly.*] What did Dr. Flack say about your arm?

LITTERLY.

Rubbed stuff into it and made a frightful fuss.

NOELINE.

Oh, there isn't any danger, is there?

LITTERLY.

Not the slightest—right in a week.

NOELINE.

[*Coldly again.*] I knew there was no occasion for you to be so alarmed.

[*She walks away, he following her.*

LITTERLY.
I say, what have I done now?

NOELINE.
Aren't you *here!*

LITTERLY.
I came after Tweenwayes and De Grival. I didn't expect *this* would happen.

NOELINE.
As it *has* happened, you might have had the decency to shower your kisses on that woman in the cupboard!

LITTERLY.
I would have done so if I'd thought that you——

NOELINE.
Oh, I don't protest against the vulgar exhibition on my own account, but I have young brothers——

LITTERLY.
I kissed her with a motive——

NOELINE.
I'm sorry to hear it.

LITTERLY.
My old nurse's daughter——!

NOELINE.
Fudge!

LITTERLY.
Known her all my life!

NOELINE.

Do your sisters kiss the head-gardener's sons?

LITTERLY.

Yes. No! [*Following her.*] I say!
[*They sit together on the settee, wrangling.*]

THOMASIN.

[*To* SHUTER] Come now, Sergeant, you might oblige a chap! They've been on the roof since six o'clock.

SHUTER.

I'd ring the alarm bell first! How am *I* to get a bottle of wine?

THOMASIN.

You could wheedle it out of old Parker.

WILHELMINA.

Do, Shuter, darling! [*Taking her arm coaxingly.*] Monsieur de Grival is such a brave fellow.

THOMASIN.

So's Tweeny!

SHUTER.

If I foraged for refreshment for *anybody* it would be for his lordship over there.

THOMASIN.

Litterly!

WILHELMINA.

We'll give Lord Litterly his share—do!

SHUTER.

M'lords, if I fetch you some refreshments will you promise me faithfully to get into that cupboard and stop there till I come back?

ALL.

Yes.

SHUTER.

No, no, not all of you! Only my young gentlemen!

NOELINE.

We understand, Sergeant.

WILHELMINA.

Of course we will.

THOMASIN.

Good man!

SHUTER.

Into the cupboard then! Into the cupboard!
 [*The three girls hurry into the cupboard and close the door.* SHUTER *unlocks the door that leads from the room.*

LITTERLY.

[*Going to her.*] I say, Letty, 'pon my word you're a good sort.

SHUTER.

I wouldn't do this for any living soul but you, m'lord.
 [*She waits, wiping her lips. He hesitates, annoyed, then kisses her. As he does so, the cupboard door opens and* NOELINE *looks out.*

K

NOELINE.

[*To herself, indignantly.*] Ah! [*As* SHUTER *departs,* LITTERLY *turns and sees* NOELINE.] Oh!
[*She withdraws her head.*

LITTERLY.

[*To himself.*] Spotted! Just my luck!

DE GRIVAL.

[*Excitedly.*] Ha, Tweenwayes, my friend! we are on the clover! [*Sitting at the piano.*] Ha, I enjoy myself like a deuce!
[*He plays, rattling off a gay French melody.*

TWEENWAYES.

[*To himself.*] Thomasin is undoubtedly beginning to regard me with great warmth! I've never felt quite like this in my life; there's nothing I'm not capable of! [*Leaping on to the horizontal bar and swinging to and fro a few times, then crying out in pain, helplessly.*] Oh! Litterly! Quick!

LITTERLY.

[*Going to him and taking him down.*] Hurt yourself, Tweeny?

TWEENWAYES.

Heavens, yes!
[*He walks in a stooping posture to the settee and sits, doubled-up.* LITTERLY *knocks at the cupboard door.*

LITTERLY.

Lady Noeline! Lady Noeline!

NOELINE.
[*From within.*] What do you want?

LITTERLY.
Please let me explain!

NOELINE.
[*Opening the door, haughtily.*] Pray don't think that any explanation is necessary.

LITTERLY.
You see, if I didn't make it right with Letty Shuter——!

NOELINE.
Oh! [*Coming out of the cupboard, in her cloak, shutting the door behind her.*] Oh, how I long for a quarter to eight. Overcote—the park—our gym.—I feel that nothing will ever be the same again!
[*Pacing about, he following her protestingly.*

THOMASIN.
[*Popping her head out of the cupboard.*] Here, Noel!

NOELINE.
Go back, Tommy, at once!

THOMASIN.
I like that! [*Coming out, in her cloak, shutting the door behind her and walking across to* TWEENWAYES.] Sneak!

NOELINE.
[*Laying her head on the vaulting horse, despairingly.*]

You see how I am treated! Oh, I wish I could undo the past few days!

LITTERLY.

Here! I say! Don't cry——!
[*They sit together on the vaulting horse.*

WILHELMINA.

[*Putting her head out of the cupboard.*] Tommy! you know I can't bear the dark!

DE GRIVAL.

Ah, Wilhelmina! Ah, my pretty girl!

WILHELMINA.

No, no!
[*He takes her hand and brings her out of the cupboard. She is in her cloak.* THOMASIN *and* TWEENWAYES *walk to-and-fro.*

TWEENWAYES.

I assure you, Lady Thomasin, I attach no importance whatever to the slight affray. We—we——

THOMASIN.

Slight! The poacher carried a loaded stick, Fitton said.

TWEENWAYES.

Possibly. Yes, I remember dashing it aside.

THOMASIN.

Lucky for old Fitton you and De Grival were on the spot.

TWEENWAYES.

[*Annoyed.*] De Grival!

THOMASIN.

Yes, didn't he――?

TWEENWAYES.

[*Waving his hand disdainfully.*] My dear Lady Thomasin!

THOMASIN.

Why, Fitton gave us to understand――

TWEENWAYES.

That De Grival――! Really!
[*They walk away as* WILHELMINA *and* DE GRIVAL *come forward talking together.*

WILHELMINA.

Ah, Monsieur de Grival, we—my sisters and I—can't thank you sufficiently.

DE GRIVAL.

Ah, please no—it thanks itself. Besides, how small a thing to do!

WILHELMINA.

To save a man's life! Why, perhaps but for Tweenwayes and yourself, Fitton would have been――

DE GRIVAL.

Tweenwayes!

WILHELMINA.

Tweenwayes assisted you, Fitton told us.

DE GRIVAL.
Ha! I laugh!
WILHELMINA.
But Fitton said——
DE GRIVAL.
Absurd! I describe it. Fitton was on the ground, with no sense, when I kick him.

WILHELMINA.
When you kicked whom?

DE GRIVAL.
Fitton.
WILHELMINA.
You kicked poor Fitton?

DE GRIVAL.
No, no, I mean Tweenwayes.

WILHELMINA.
Why should you kick Tweenwayes?

DE GRIVAL.
Ah, I am not telling it! I—I—kick them all! Don'cher know!
[*The attention of* DE GRIVAL *and* WILHELMINA, TWEENWAYES *and* THOMASIN *is attracted by* NOELINE *and* LITTERLY, *who are sitting on the vaulting horse, their heads are close together and* LITTERLY'S *arm placed lightly round* NOELINE'S *waist.*

THOMASIN.

Noel!

WILHELMINA.

Oh, Noel!

THOMASIN.

Lord Litterly!
[LITTERLY *and* NOELINE *hastily dismount and face the others.*

LITTERLY.

Eh? What—what?

THOMASIN.

[*Listening.*] Hark! Here's the Sergeant! Get back! get back!

WILHELMINA.

[*In a terrified whisper.*] Oh, I didn't know I was out!
[*The three girls hurriedly return to the cupboard;* LITTERLY *throws himself full length on to the settee and whistles unconcernedly,* DE GRIVAL *resumes his seat at the piano, playing with much energy;* TWEENWAYES *rushes to the horizontal bar and hangs there, without motion.* SHUTER *enters, carrying a tray on which are a bottle of hock, some glasses, and a cake.* LITTERLY *rises, takes the tray from her, and places it on the table.* SHUTER *relocks the door and looks round suspiciously, then she finds* WILHELMINA'S *shoe which, in the scurry, has been dropped.*

SHUTER.

[*Picking up the shoe.*] Ah, the deceitful young devils! [*She opens the cupboard door;* NOELINE *re-enters the room;* THOMASIN *following her.* WILHELMINA *appears, timidly, searching for her shoe.* SHUTER *produces it.*] You've been out!

WILHELMINA.

I must have been!

THOMASIN.

[*Coming between* SHUTER *and* WILHELMINA.] Now then! Willy wasn't the first to break our promise. *I* was!

NOELINE.

Nothing of the kind! *I* was! How presuming you are, Tommy!

SHUTER.

Oh, you—you—you bad lot! You——!
[LITTERLY *has filled the glasses, and now advances with the tray.*

LITTERLY.

Now, now, now! We're all going to drink Letty Shuter's health.

SHUTER.

[*Mollified.*] Oh, m'lord——!
[LITTERLY *hands the tray from one to the other.*

TWEENWAYES.

[*To* WILHELMINA.] After such stirring adventures, a glass of champagne is particularly acceptable.

WILHELMINA.
It isn't champagne; it's our dinner hock.

TWEENWAYES.
[*To himself, bitterly.*] We hate hock!
[*He sits moodily. The girls place* SHUTER *upon the vaulting-horse.*

LITTERLY.
Now! Bumpers! We drink long life and a second husband to Letitia Ann Shuter!

THOMASIN.
Letitia Ann Shuter! Good man!

WILHELMINA *and* NOELINE.
Sergeant!

ALL.
Sergeant Shuter!
[*The toast is drunk with acclamation.*

DE GRIVAL.
[*At the piano again, excitedly.*] Ah, we are having a good time! If we danced we should like it.

THOMASIN.
Yes, yes! Sergeant, rattle off something for us!

WILHELMINA.
Oh, no!

NOELINE.
Tommy, be quiet!

THOMASIN.

"Binding the Wheatsheaf"! The old dance we dug up at Drumdurris!

WILHELMINA.

Oh, yes! Shuter knows that!
[SHUTER *takes* DE GRIVAL'S *place at the piano*.

TWEENWAYES.

[*Putting on some torn and soiled gloves.*] We—we are no dancers.

[*They dance a quaint country-dance, beginning demurely and increasing in energy as they proceed.* DE GRIVAL *is dancing alone, very wildly and fantastically, when the door opens and* LADY CASTLEJORDAN, *who has apparently opened the door with a key attached to her chatelaine, enters with* MINCHIN. LADY CASTLEJORDAN *stands as if stricken; gradually the dancers fall back, with the exception of* DE GRIVAL, *who does not see* LADY CASTLEJORDAN *and continues dancing. Then he discovers his position and bolts into the cupboard.* LADY CASTLEJORDAN *sinks upon the settee, looking before her with a fixed stare, and sitting motionless.* SHUTER *is still playing gaily;* MINCHIN *goes to her and taps her upon the shoulder; she stops playing, turns, rises, looks round, and totters out at the door.*

LADY CASTLEJORDAN.

What is it? Roger Minchin! I'm going mad, I think. What is it?

MINCHIN.

Lady Noeline, you are the eldest of three, I still hope, not altogether worthless young women. But, upon my word, unless you instantly furnish some reasonable explanation of the presence of these gentlemen I shall find myself guilty of wishing that you had never been born.

NOELINE.

Mother, this is—my cousin—your nephew——
[LITTERLY *comes forward.*

LADY CASTLEJORDAN.

[*Staring at him.*] What's that you say?

NOELINE.

Lord Litterly rendered me a great service in London, though I didn't know till this afternoon to whom I was indebted for it.

LADY CASTLEJORDAN.

That young man at Overcote!

NOELINE.

He came here to restore me a ring I had lost; he didn't find out until he had entered the park that he was at Overcote.

LADY CASTLEJORDAN.

Cannot he make his own excuses?

LITTERLY.

No, Lady Castlejordan, I can't, and I—I—I say, aunt Miriam——

LADY CASTLEJORDAN.

Stand away! Who are the others? There are others!

THOMASIN.

Mater—mater—Lord Tweenwayes—begs me to present him to you.

LADY CASTLEJORDAN.

Tweenwayes——?

[TWEENWAYES, *who has been under the vaulting-horse, is now half-way up the rope. He bows from that elevated position.*

TWEENWAYES.

Lady Castlejordan, I rejoice to find myself at Overcote Hall. We—we——

LADY CASTLEJORDAN.

[*To* THOMASIN.] I see! The result of your stay at Drumdurris under Egidia's care! I am mightily obliged to her!

TWEENWAYES.

I take the present opportunity——

MINCHIN.

[*Enraged.*] Come down!

[TWEENWAYES *descends rapidly.*

WILHELMINA.

[*Faintly.*] Mother dear—Monsieur de Grival——

LADY CASTLEJORDAN.

[*Raising her head.*] What! the other!

WILHELMINA.

[*Looking around.*] André! André!
[MINCHIN *opens the outer door and calls* DE GRIVAL. *No one appears.* *The others call* DE GRIVAL *with the same result.* LITTERLY *enters the cupboard indignantly ; there is a short pause and then* DE GRIVAL *is shot out into the centre of the room.* LITTERLY *re-enters more leisurely.*

LADY CASTLEJORDAN.

[*Glaring at* DE GRIVAL.] So that is—the Frenchman?

DE GRIVAL.

French by birth, yes. But so long educated in England: English in my appearance, manner, voice—English to my backbone. Do I not play your games, follow your sport——?

MINCHIN *and* LITTERLY.

Hush! hush!

WILHELMINA.

[*To* DE GRIVAL, *presenting him formally.*] Monsieur André De Grival—Lady Castlejordan, my mother.

DE GRIVAL.

[*With a profound bow.*] Ah, Lady Castlejordan, damitall! [*There is a general protest of* "*No!*"

MINCHIN.

Upon my soul, sir——!

DE GRIVAL.

Ah, I do not say the right word! I mistake it! I despair!

MINCHIN *and* LITTERLY.

Hush! hush!

DE GRIVAL.

I rave madly! To-night I stab my throat! Don' cher know!

WILHELMINA.

Oh! [DE GRIVAL *is dragged back by* LITTERLY.

LADY CASTLEJORDAN.

[*Rising.*] Roger Minchin, I wish to speak to my eldest child. Take these gentlemen away for a few moments. [MINCHIN *beckons the men, who quietly retire into the cupboard.*] Noel! [MINCHIN *places a chair for* LADY CASTLEJORDAN.] Noel, I went to town to receive a statement from Florence Vipont's maid, Dawkins.

NOELINE.

Oh! Treacherous creature!

LADY CASTLEJORDAN.

The woman declares you sallied out the other night in young Robert Vipont's clothes. Is it true?

NOELINE.

Perfectly. Surely *you* can have no objection to such a proceeding, mother?

LADY CASTLEJORDAN.

Noel!

MINCHIN.

[*Shaking a finger at* LADY CASTLEJORDAN.] Hah!

LADY CASTLEJORDAN.

But you didn't return till early morning, according to Dawkins. You've never heard me say I like *that* in a young man!

NOELINE.

No, mother, but I got mixed up in a street-fight, through protecting a girl from a brute who was going to hit her. I punched him, mother!

LADY CASTLEJORDAN.

What?

MINCHIN.

You did?

LADY CASTLEJORDAN.

In the public street? Before people?

NOELINE.

You've had me taught to do such things!

MINCHIN.

Hah!

LADY CASTLEJORDAN.

In the presence of strangers—never!

NOELINE.

After I'd done it I ran away, and fainted in a by-turning.

LADY CASTLEJORDAN.

Fainted! My—son!

NOELINE.

But, luckily, Lord Litterly came along and picked me up and carried me home to his lodgings——

LADY CASTLEJORDAN.

Oh! My daughter!
[MINCHIN *joins* WILHELMINA *and* THOMASIN, *and talks with them.*

NOELINE.

This morning he recognised me in Chesham Street and followed me here to return a ring I'd dropped in his room.

LADY CASTLEJORDAN.

[*Pacing to and fro.*] Disgraceful! disgraceful!

NOELINE.

Yes, mother, it is disgraceful! But it will serve everybody a good turn if it teaches us that, after all, your children are nothing but ordinary, weak, affectionate, chicken-hearted young women!

LADY CASTLEJORDAN.

Noel!

NOELINE.

[*Stamping her foot.*] No! Noeline from this moment! Noeline! Noeline!

MINCHIN.

Lady Castlejordan, I really think it due to Lord Tweenwayes and Monsieur de Grival that you should know they have stood you in good stead during your absence.

LADY CASTLEJORDAN.

Mr. Minchin?

MINCHIN.

As the result of their perfectly inexcusable presence in your park, old Fitton the keeper has been rescued from the murderous clutches of a most determined poacher——

THOMASIN.

Quite true, mater—Tweenwayes may be bred a bit too fine, but, in an emergency, he's a demon.

WILHELMINA.

You should hear what Fitton says of André.

MINCHIN.

I'll enquire about this. [*He goes out.*

LADY CASTLEJORDAN.

Fitton or no Fitton, this shameful introduction of men into Overcote——!

THOMASIN.

If we're boys, we must have pals!

WILHELMINA.

The misery is we're neither one thing nor the other!

LADY CASTLEJORDAN.

In the gymnasium! Dancing! [*Looking round.*] And drinking!

L

THOMASIN.

A bottle of Rüdesheimer. If one man can't give another a glass of wine——!

LADY CASTLEJORDAN.

[*Furiously.*] Into your frocks! Into your frocks!

WILHELMINA, THOMASIN *and* NOELINE.

Frocks!

LADY CASTLEJORDAN.

Into your frocks! [*Sinking into the chair.*] And never, never, never come out of them!

[THOMASIN *and* WILHELMINA *go to the door.*

WILHELMINA.

[*Sobbing.*] I—I—I've felt ashamed of my appearance for ever so long! I own it. [*She goes out.*

THOMASIN.

[*Rebelliously.*] All right, turn me into a girl! But, look here, I shall be just the sort of young lady that's likely to be an awful failure in the end! [*She goes out.*

NOELINE.

[*Pointing to the cupboard.*] Mother, don't forget they're in there.

LADY CASTLEJORDAN.

Ah, I had forgotten.

NOELINE.

I—I hope you'll—like Litterly.

LADY CASTLEJORDAN.

You hope I will like—[*suddenly*] do *you* ?

NOELINE.

Yes. [*She goes out.*]

LADY CASTLEJORDAN.

Noeline! Come back! Is it possible! My brain reels! [*She goes to the door, opens and shuts it, then goes and opens the cupboard door, calling sternly.*] Lord Tweenwayes—Monsieur de Grival—Lord Litterly. [TWEENWAYES *appears, encounters* LADY CASTLEJORDAN *and retreats.*] Lord Tweenwayes!

> [TWEENWAYES *appears again, bows apprehensively to* Lady CASTLEJORDAN, *and sidles round the cupboard door.* DE GRIVAL *enters, bows to* LADY CASTLEJORDAN, *and edging away from her, joins* TWEENWAYES. LITTERLY *enters.*

LITTERLY.

[*Meekly.*] You desire to——?

LADY CASTLEJORDAN.

To demand that you instantly leave Overcote and to tell you that I can find no words in which——

LITTERLY.

Aunt Miriam——!

LADY CASTLEJORDAN.

Aunt! How dare you remind me of our relationship! How dare you——!

[*Pausing and staring at him.*

LITTERLY.
Eh? You're not well——

LADY CASTLEJORDAN.
Have you ever been told that you have your late uncle's eyes?

LITTERLY.
My father often says I recall his brother Jack.

LADY CASTLEJORDAN.
Why, if your hair wasn't quite so short—and if it was curly just there—and if you were an inch taller—and hadn't such an odious town air—oh!
[*She grasps his arms impulsively, then falls back with an exclamation.*

LITTERLY.
Aunt!

LADY CASTLEJORDAN.
[*Again grasping his arms.*] Pardon me! [*Leaving him.*] Mercy! His muscles are like my Jack's!

MINCHIN *enters.*

MINCHIN.
[*To* LADY CASTLEJORDAN.] My dear Lady Castlejordan, Fitton happened to be in the game-larder. He certainly has told me a story of almost incredible dash and presence of mind on the part of Lord Tweenwayes and Monsieur de Grival——

LADY CASTLEJORDAN.
[*To* MINCHIN.] Yes, yes, yes. Mr. Minchin, don't

you see an extraordinary likeness in Litterly to my Jack?

MINCHIN.

There is a suggestion——

LADY CASTLEJORDAN.

A suggestion! Mr. Minchin, what—what ought I to do? [*A deep gong sounds in the distance.*]

MINCHIN.

Dinner! What ought you to do? Begin at once to distract your girls' thoughts from the follies of the past! Demonstrate with as little delay as possible that you can be a reasonable mother! [*Glancing towards the men.*] Ask 'em to dine.

LADY CASTLEJORDAN.

What!

MINCHIN.

They're all more or less injured; they must be all more or less hungry; be more or less hospitable.

LADY CASTLEJORDAN.

No, no; if I ask anybody it shall be only Litterly.

MINCHIN.

Why only Litterly?

LADY CASTLEJORDAN.

He's so like my Jack! He's so like my Jack!

MINCHIN.

You can't invite one blackguard without the others.

LADY CASTLEJORDAN.

A blackguard! When he is so like my Jack!

NOELINE, WILHELMINA, and THOMASIN *enter, dressed in demi-toilette for dinner.*

MINCHIN.

[*Triumphantly.*] Hah! hah!

LADY CASTLEJORDAN

[*To* MINCHIN, *proudly.*] Oh, yes, aren't they beautiful girls! [*Addressing the three men.*] Lord Tweenwayes, Lord Litterly, Monsieur de Grival, as you see, I am still in my early-morning gown. On the score of dress therefore I beg you will have no hesitation in giving me the honour of your company at dinner.

[*The girls, uttering little cries, sit suddenly upon the settee.*

TWEENWAYES.

Lady Castlejordan——!

DE GRIVAL.

Ah, I shall delight to eat!

LITTERLY.

You're very good, my dear aunt!

[*The girls rise and gather round their mother kissing and embracing her.*

NOELINE.

Oh, mother!

WILHELMINA.

Mother dear!

THOMASIN.

Good business!
[LITTERLY *and* MINCHIN *meet and shake hands.*

DE GRIVAL.

[*Flourishing the Indian clubs.*] La, la, la!

TWEENWAYES.

[*Swinging on the horizontal bar.*] We carry everything before us! [*The gong sounds again,*

LADY CASTLEJORDAN.

Lord Tweenwayes—
[TWEENWAYES *comes with great dignity to* LADY CASTLEJORDAN. *The girls fall back.*

LADY CASTLEJORDAN.

Lord Litterly—Lady Noeline. Monsieur de Grival—Lady Wilhelmina. Mr. Minchin—Lady Thomasin.
[*The couples are formed, and all go out sedately.*

THE END.

Printed by BALLANTYNE, HANSON & CO.
London & Edinburgh.

www.ingramcontent.com/pod-product-compliance
Lightning Source LLC
Chambersburg PA
CBHW031447160426
43195CB00010BB/880